The Merchant Adventurers

The Merchant Adventurers

A Family History

The Golden Hind by Bernard Finnegan Gribble
(An English sixteenth-century sailing vessel,
courtesy of Nick Gribble and Poole Museum)

MARGARET DAVISON

THE CHOIR PRESS

Copyright © 2023 Margaret Davison

All rights reserved. No part of this publication may be reproduced or transmitted in any form or by any means, electronic or mechanical including photocopying, recording or any information storage or retrieval system, without prior permission in writing from the publishers.

The right of Margaret Davison to be identified as the author of this work has been asserted by her in accordance with the Copyright, Designs and Patents Act 1988

First published in the United Kingdom in 2023 by
The Choir Press

ISBN 978-1-78963-340-5

Dedication

To
Sarah and Christopher
&
in loving remembrance of Susan and Sharon

Contents

Acknowledgement	ix
Preface	xi
Introduction	xiii
John Johnson ca. 1514-1590	1
A Merchant's Path to Success	4
Richard De Whytmere (Whitmore) 1495–1549	7
William Whitmore 1525–1593	12
Apprenticeship	16
The Merchant Years	21
Trading in Spain	23
William Bond 1524–1576	35
William Bond and Margaret Aldy – Who They Were	37
William Bond – The Merchant's Tale	40
William Bond (the younger) ca. 1555–1608/09	58
Simon Bourman b. ca. 1525/30–1601	63
The Spanish Armada 1588	71
Martin Bond 1558–1643	77
Netherland Merchants	84
Reginald/Reynold Copcott 1546–1598	85
Richard Daniell 1561–1630	95
Epilogue	105
Notes	111
Index	113

Acknowledgements

My grateful thanks, first and foremost to my husband, Michael for his unstinting encouragement and patient help, especially in times of doubt. To my cousin Jennie Marshall whose interest in family history and stories heard in childhood inspired me to bring these historical characters to life. Without Michael and Jennie this history might never have been written.

Thanks are also due to Nick Gribble for permission to use the beautiful painting of the Golden Hind by Bernard Gribble, and to Geoff Cryer for allowing the use of his artistic photograph of Apley Hall (see https://geoffspages.blog/).

I am also very grateful to Dr. Christopher Moran and Emily Rae for providing me with information and photographs of the renewed Crosby Hall, once the home of the Bond family and now known as Crosby Moran Hall. Raising Crosby Hall from ignoble decrepitude has been a lifelong labour of love for Dr. Moran. His awareness of the significance of history has provided the nation with a glimpse into Tudor life and architecture that we would not otherwise have.

Lastly, thank you to The Choir Press for helping me bring this book to fruition and particulartly to David Onyett, Joshua Lambert, Adrian Sysum and Rachel Woodman for their help with editing and printing this book.

Acknowledgments

Merchant Adventurers's Arms

Preface

The Merchant Adventurers of the 15th and 16thC were a group of merchants belonging to the Company of Merchant Adventurers of London who initially exported wool to the Netherlands and Calais in return for other commodities and then branched forth to form trading Companies in a number of other countries across the globe – Russia, the Levant, Spain and East India. They faced considerable adversity, first from the Hanseatic merchants who traded with unfair privileges until these were revoked and then much disruption from the Spanish intent on imposing their Catholic faith and threatening the English throne.

In a bid to beat competitors they financed expeditions by, Sir Hugh Willoughby, Richard Chancellor, and Martin Frobisher to find and explore sea passages to the Orient via a Northeast and Northwest Passage.

These adventurers became politically and internationally important as advisers and financiers to the monarchs of their time through their understanding of other cultures and people, international politics, languages and coinage. They knew what was going on and reported accordingly. Their success changed England. The nation gradually moved from a feudal state of serfdom to the nascent capitalist structures of the Renaissance. Wealth was no longer vested in the aristocracy because the successful merchant adventurers were extremely rich and powerful. Their money was needed and enabled many aspects of life to move forward. Old and new rich lived and worked in a symbiotic relationship. This is the story and insight into Tudor life that this book describes.

Introduction

The Norman system of primogeniture gave rise to the establishment of the English aristocracy and gentry. It was among this group and across a time span of around nearly 1,000 years that some of these families and their kin entered the annals of history. This book aims to tell the story of the merchant adventurers from the sixteenth-century paternal and maternal lines of these connected families and those related to them. It also aims to make clear their genealogical history, providing more than the usual number of dates so the many people across the world, who believe they are descendants can follow their own genealogy more easily. The story weaves across the historical events through which they lived, describing how their fortunes ebbed and flowed according to the tides of religious conflict, politics and battles, and the difficulties they encountered as they ventured forth to trade across Europe, Russia and Newfoundland.

The start of the sixteenth century brought to a close the mediaeval period. The later years of the Tudor age became an age of transformation. It heralded the birth of a future navy and a growth in commerce born from a natural curiosity to learn what lay beyond the shores of Britain and Europe. This drove forth exploration, the finding of new lands and trading opportunities. As a result, the English eventually traded across the globe to control an empire. Whereas the familial links of the past had been for the most part parochial, from the sixteenth century onwards they came from many parts of Britain and occasionally elsewhere, drawn together by commerce and government.

This colourful and adventurous epoch widened England's influence and commercial enterprise throughout the world but, as will be seen, the sixteenth and seventeenth centuries also became periods dominated by religious upheaval in Europe and Britain. That created difficulties for the commodity markets. If Britain was to succeed in the highly competitive European stage, the merchant adventurers also had to overcome competition, especially from the Hansa merchants and the seafaring and financially superior Dutch and Spanish nations.

John Johnson ca. 1514–1590

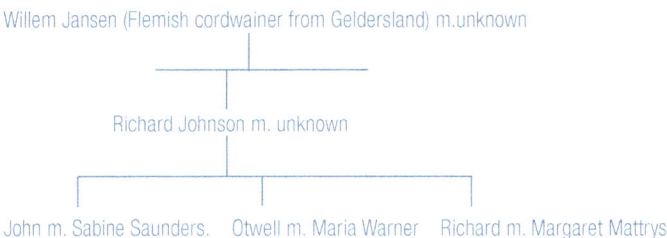

Events during his lifetime:

- 1514 Thomas Wolsey starts to build his home, Hampton Court
- 1515 Katherine of Aragon, wife of Henry VIII, gives birth to future Queen Mary
- 1524 William Tyndale plans to translate the Bible into English
- 1542 Catherine Howard, fifth wife of Henry VIII executed
- 1551 Outbreak of Sweating Sickness
- 1553 Mary Tudor crowned Queen Mary I
- 1560 Tobacco grown in Europe for medicinal purposes
- 1589 Clergyman William Lee develops first industrial machinery to knit stockings

Each merchant had to overcome commercial setbacks and physical perils, any of which could jeopardise trading livelihoods.

One victim of unexpected circumstance was the handsome, auburn-haired John Johnson of Dutch/Flemish descent, a sixteenth-century merchant of the Drapers Company. He and his brother Otwell had a successful business at the Calais staple where they had a counting house within the home of their aunt Margaret Baynham whose stepdaughter was married to John's factor, Humphrey Lightfoot. Here they traded cloth, herring, grain, wine and other commodities, affording them a comfortable lifestyle and country estates in England in keeping with their many affluent relations.

Highly literate in both written and spoken English, French and Flemish, the Johnson family's correspondence is an intriguing insight into their family life, health, outbreaks of plague, religious conflict in England and the Netherlands, the mercantile trade of Calais, and the events of their time. Otwell writes of his shock at witnessing the execution of Catherine Howard and her lady-in-waiting, Lady Rochford after Henry VIII discovered his queen's infidelity. Otwell had helped with the arrangements for the execution because Sir John Gage, with whom

Otwell worked, was the constable of the Tower of London, responsible for such events. The martyrdom in 1555 of John Johnson's brother-in-law, Laurence Saunders, his closest friend and the much-loved brother of John's wife, Sabine was a particular sorrow. The children of the family were devoted to this kind and gentle man who refused to recant his Protestant faith. Queen Mary I, a keen Catholic, persecuted Protestants and, after Laurence had preached against the re-introduction of Mass, she demanded that Laurence be burnt at the stake.[1]

As revealed by the Johnson letters and other papers, the Calais merchants were a close-knit community of interconnected families. Through his wife Sabine, John Johnson had several relatives related to the other adventurers of this history, such as Copcott and Whitmore. In addition, Blaise (Blaze) Saunders, another brother of Sabine, is mentioned in the will of the adventurer William Bond. William Bond probably knew him through their mercantile trade and the aldermanry as both were common councillors and lived in Bishopsgate. As well as his other activities, Blaise was the official garbler for the port of Calais; that is, he was responsible for assuring the quality of spices and drugs coming into the port.

All these Calais merchants, supportive of each other, had become successful, rich and powerful as their wills demonstrate. Misfortune, however, sometimes caused a disastrous divergence from triumph. A new and lethal disease had arisen in 1484. Over a span of about seventy years it re-occurred every ten years or so, claiming the lives of thousands, some so rapidly that it was said, '*a man may be merry at dinner and dead at supper.*'

1551 became *annus horribilis* for the flourishing and amiable Johnson family. Having lain dormant for twenty-three years this disease, the Sweating Sickness returned. John Johnson's younger brother, Otwell, the manager of the family business and the most able and astute of the three brothers, fell prey to this dreaded disease. A good business can survive one or two setbacks but a culmination of factors may prove impossible to overcome.

That year brought economic chaos as well as disease. Henry VIII had incurred colossal debt as a result of battles with the French and a lavish lifestyle. It led to a debasement of the English coinage, a rise in the cost of living and caused a fall in the rate of exchange. Inevitably, many merchants suffered financially. The fall in the rate of exchange meant merchants owed more than they received yet debts had to be honoured. The merchants in

---

[1] Laurence Saunders, educated at Eton and King's College, Cambridge, was initially apprenticed to merchant Sir William Chester but returned to university where he obtained a doctorate in theology.

Calais and the Antwerp staple demanded gold rather than the debased value of England's coins. Consequently, gold, the fall-back currency, became scarce and expensive. Fearful about debt and the lowering of prices, many letters flowed between John, his youngest brother Richard Johnston and Anthony Cave with whom the Johnsons operated. Several of the merchants' letters make clear the difficulty in acquiring ships for their freight and the obstruction to trade due to political intransigence. The ensuing problems were made worse by Richard Johnson. After Otwell's death, Richard Johnson, based in Calais, compounded the financial predicament besetting the Johnson business by incompetence and muddled bookkeeping. The honest, hard-working and sensible John Johnson might have succeeded but for his brother's lack of acumen. Misfortune does not discriminate between the deserving and undeserving.

That autumn, in desperation, John Johnson hired two ships to carry wine from Spain. Several vessels arrived in English ports, the first being Blaise Saunder's ship. The days and weeks passed but of Johnson's vessels and cargo there was no sign. Then word arrived that French warships had attacked and plundered the two ships stealing their equipment; sails, anchors; ... everything removable. They even divested the sailors of their clothing. After a heroic endeavour to preserve his business, John Johnson and his glamorous wife, Sabine, finally lost everything to bankruptcy and had to leave their much-loved Glapthorne estate in Northamptonshire. The help of friends and family and one or two intermittent jobs were all that lay between them and the abyss of poverty. This likeable, brave pair sustained each other and their children amid considerable anxiety for twenty years, proving their love, resilience and ingenuity in adversity until, at last, William Cecil, now Lord Burghley, came to the rescue. With his influence, John became the official clerk of the Merchants' Staple Company and his youngest son, Edward was appointed under-clerk. Sir Francis Walsingham also gave some support. At last, the years in the wilderness were over; John Johnson's ceaseless efforts were repaid and the family, sons, daughters and grandchildren, found renewed hope. That so many merchants, including those of this history, bequeathed money to debtors prisons, highlights their understanding of how precarious life and business could be.

Like so many others in fear of their lives, John Johnson and Sabine fled England in 1551. First they went to Bruges and then to Calais, but the tentacles of disease reached Calais too. John and Sabine fell prey but this robust pair were among the survivors.

Several hypotheses have been suggested as to the cause of the sweating sickness, including hantavirus pulmonary syndrome, which causes fever and haemorrhage. In 2004 a new hypothesis suggested that anthrax spores inhaled from contaminated wool might have been the culprit, but neither entirely fit the symptoms as described – apprehension, rigor, dizziness, headache, exhaustion and severe pains in the upper torso and limbs. To this day, medical science has failed to solve the mystery of the disease that more often affected young and affluent men. Strangely, after 1551, this wretched disease was never to return.

A Tudor Family Portrait by Barbara Winchester[2] gives a more detailed and fascinating account of the Johnsons, their kin, the families of Cave, Saxby and Saunders and their friends. It describes the Calais merchants and life at court, including the martyrdom, by Mary I, of the Eton-educated Laurence Saunders, Sabine's brother, for preaching against the Catholic Church.

A Merchant's Path to Success

John and Otwell Johnson had been highly successful merchants until a series of misfortunes beyond John's control made it impossible for him to carry on. Even if his younger brother had been competent, the monetary chaos had made life very difficult for all but the wealthiest. What then, apart from financial security, were the components that made some merchants so successful against the odds?

Besides overcoming problems of money supply and the vagaries of political strife at home or abroad, factors over which they had little control, the merchants' success depended upon a collection of skills, ability and hard work. As well as being personable and intelligent, they needed a detailed knowledge of their trade, the coinage of the countries with which they traded, the exchange rates, aptitude for management and communication in order to liaise with their agents abroad, and an entrepreneurial approach. They also had to provide a good training for their apprentices with whom they may liaise or partner at a later date.

Changes in circumstances required a fast response as well as a detailed record of financial transactions at a time when there were no banks. Merchants had to foresee the possible outcome of political events within their own country and those with which they had dealings. They needed the resources to withstand loss of trade, whether by theft, piracy or storms and have consideration towards their agents and factors working for them overseas. In the absence of banks, trust between merchants was essential.

---

[2] A Tudor Family Portrait by Barbara Winchester, created from her doctorate thesis, '*The Johnson letters 1542–52*' (unpublished University of London Ph.D. thesis, 1953)

Large quantities of coinage would be impossible to carry and that necessitated the issuing of bills of exchange and promissory pay notes. The Company of Merchant Adventurers was formed to help protect these merchants' interests.

Thus, the minutiae of all transactions had to be recorded in meticulous detail within correspondence books and double entry ledgers, a laborious but vital task, at which Richard Johnson had been so inept. Other essentials were a rigorous level of social skills as demanded by the mores of Tudor etiquette and society. The entrepreneurial ability of these 'merchant princes' and their raising of funds for merchandising became one of the means by which England established her international lead in trade, which hitherto had been held by the Venetians and Portuguese.

The adventurers three-masted vessels included barques, brigs and carracks. Some of these were armed for long voyages and, when required, they augmented the navy to wrest mastery of the seas from the might of the Spanish, Dutch and Portuguese navies.

Educated and fluent in writing and speech in up to four languages, including Latin, merchants had the contacts to sell at a very handsome profit. The establishment of large warehouses enabled them to store their wares in bulk, permitting trade on a far greater scale with greater profit than in the past. With such profit the merchants could act as bankers for commercial purposes and provide loans to impoverished peers and the crown. They were a needed resource in the absence of lending banks. The forerunner of the English banking system, the Medici Bank of London, had folded in debt in 1478, partly through merchants having their own system, but also because many debts remained unhonoured.

These merchants steered England's place within the commercial markets of Europe and overcame the superior monetary system of the Dutch. In so doing they became the new aristocracy, though some were of ancient lineage anyway. They helped to propel the vibrant social change that took place during the Tudor and early Stuart reigns. No longer could the old aristocracy remain aloof, holding commerce and those who worked for a living in disdain. Living beyond their means, these peers needed the new rich to fund their debts and marry their sons and daughters. The merchants' knowledge of other nations' trade, culture and politics enabled them and their descendants to act as administrators, advisers and governors of the English realm and her dominions, and become useful confidantes, advisers and financiers to the English monarchs of their era. The British and similar-thinking Dutch bourgeoisie held the reins that guided their nations to a prosperous posterity. This merchant class changed living standards, and status, as much as the famine and plague of the fourteenth century had raised the surviving peasants to the yeomanry. Thus their lives provide us with an understanding of Elizabethan history.

The hindrances they experienced were costly to them, yet such circumstances presented opportunity for England and those prepared to take risks. Gathering clouds can offer possibilities to those with the vision to see them. The demise of Antwerp's trading centre at the hands of the Spanish allowed London to take her place. Despite political challenges, England was at peace under a strong queen and people used that advantage. Fleeing immigrants brought their skills to London where the English were quick to learn. London, its people and its merchants flourished.

But what of the merchants' wives? Like Sabine Johnson, far from being closet individuals, several were educated, and developed logistic and management skills to match those of their husbands. Using these skills, they ran the family estates, manor and workers during the absence of their menfolk, ensuring enough food and provisions to last until the next shipment of goods, which could take weeks or months. They organised and nurtured the social life of the family, thereby furthering the family's standing within the hierarchical structure of society. Sabine had been assiduous in cultivating friends and family contacts during the absence of husband John. As a young wife, she tells him of entertaining several members of the family, friends and their wives.

During illness or after the death of their husbands, some wives used their commercial knowledge to continue the family business, provide loans, acquire property and support charities in their own right. John Johnson found the support of his wife, Sabine, invaluable during times of illness and commercial disaster. His aunt,[i] the widowed Margaret Baynham of Calais ran a farm, provided board and lodging for merchants and traded in her own right between Calais and England after the death of her husband Robert, a mayor of Calais. Margaret Bond wife of William Bond of Crosby Place described later, traded with Russia and, a generation later, widows Elizabeth Craven and Frances Weld, both daughters of the adventurer William Whitmore, oversaw the education and marriages of their children. Elizabeth also bought and sold property as advised by her husband in his will. The indomitable Frances Weld used the courts to litigate for what she believed her rightful dues. In some respects, these women appear to have enjoyed greater freedom and respect than that afforded to their Victorian descendants.

Richard de Whytmere (Whitmore) 1495–1549

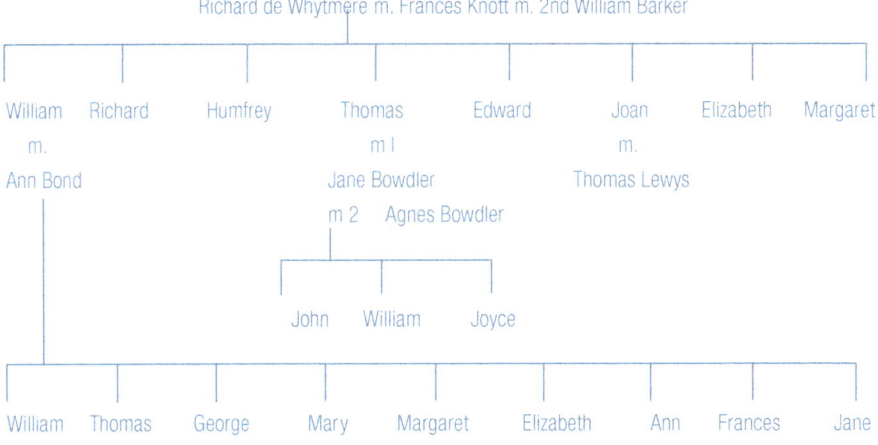

Events during his lifetime:

- 1485 Henry VII became king after the defeat of Richard III at Battle of Bosworth
- 1492 The infamous Rodrigo Borgia became Pope Alexander VI of Rome
- 1492 Columbus found America
- 1503 Leonardo da Vinci begins painting of the Mona Lisa
- 1509 1509 King Henry VII dies and reign of Henry VIII begins
- 1521 Diet of Worms – Martin Luther declared a heretic and outlawed
- King Henry VIII dies 1547

Richard de Whytmere, a yeoman farmer, was the father of the first merchant adventurer of the Whitmore family. He held land in Claverley, Shropshire, a county that came into existence as part of the Kingdom of Mercia, ruled by Offa from AD 757. Richard's ancestors, with roots tracing back to the Norman Conquest, had established themselves in this area sometime during the reign of Henry III. Descendants have lived in Shropshire ever since and this is where William Whitmore, the adventurer, spent the early years of his childhood.

Shropshire, a beautiful rural county, timeless and steeped in history, is a landscape of misted hills, deep pools and dells and gnarled, ancient woods. It is a land of legends and myths that includes a Saxon family ancestor on the maternal side of the family named Edric 'the wild' Sylvaticus, a valiant, mystical son of the Marches, an adversary and 'thorn in the flesh' of William the Conqueror, who came to admire his martial prowess. They say that on dark and stormy nights, a horseman may be seen against the skyline on the Long Mynd: wild Edric, an apparition said to be a portent of war, as once more he summons his Welsh and Saxon warriors to follow him into battle. His last recorded appearance was shortly before the Battle of Waterloo.

Not far from Claverley lies the village of Wroxeter, once the fourth largest city in Roman Britain, Viroconium Cornoviorum, currently being excavated.

Roman City at Wroxeter
Viroconium Cornoviorum

Richard's land in Claverley surrounded by narrow, winding lanes is over-hung by sandstone cliffs and caves; caves that have sheltered hermits and peasants, hidden fugitives and warriors and secreted the treasures of great mansions during times of peril. Over the centuries, castles have guarded and defended the county from Welsh invaders and sheep-rustlers. The castles are still there, some in ruins, eerie ghosts of earlier times. Others stand proud, stately and cared for as family homes and tourist attractions. Shropshire's forests, the hunting grounds of English kings, covered a large proportion of the land. According to legend, the goddess Sabrina presides over the long, pretty and sometimes powerfully dangerous River Severn that in the past enabled the flow of trade as the river wended through the counties down to the sea. As time rolled forward from the mediaeval period to the Renaissance, Shropshire's successful sons returned from the City to their origins and built grand mansions. In their footsteps others followed to enjoy the charms of a peaceful, bucolic setting of sheep-grazed pastures.

Nowadays that is not all that Shropshire has to offer. Besides the rolling hills and dells and outstanding loveliness, Shropshire has mineral resources – coal, iron ore, copper and lead. Such riches brought forth the Industrial

Revolution and gave rise to the 'satanic mills' of William Blake's poem 'Jerusalem', as well as the famous Iron Bridge built by Abraham Darby that spans the gorge at the eponymously named village of Ironbridge. But all that belongs to another story. Today, as a World Heritage Site, Shropshire offers museums, potteries, history, walks, gardens and stately homes in abundance.

Richard de Whytmere of Claverley entered the world as the mediaeval era came to a close and England stood on the cusp of a golden age of adventure and change. Richard was born in 1495 towards the end of the reign of Henry VII of England and three years after Christopher Columbus reached the New World. The reign of King Henry VIII began a few years afterwards and the infamous Florentine statesman Niccol Machiavelli outlined his political philosophy in *The Prince*.

Descended from John de Whytmere, lord of the manor of Whittemere and Bobbington in the early thirteenth century, the family now held land at Aston, Hopton and Heathton in the manor of Claverley as well as Claverley itself. These brought in revenue from farming and lease of land. Richard was comparatively well-off, a fact confirmed by his bequest to the poor of the parish and loans to a relation named Richard Billingsley.[3] His will of 1549 details the debt of 15s (equivalent to £206 in 2017) lent by him to a family member in a lending tradition that would be carried on by Richard's descendants. It was Richard who changed the family name from the Norman 'de Whytmere' to the anglicised 'Whitmore'.

In the year 1524, at the age of twenty-nine, he married Frances Knott.[ii] The Shropshire records show that a family named Knotte/Knot lived in Claverley and Frances is thought to be the daughter of Thomas Knott. He was a reeve from 1505–1506, responsible for the overall management of the village and for ensuring serfs carried out their duties. In 1473 a Richard Knotte was the priest of Claverley church and a John Knotte, a collector of rents for Claverley from 1499–1500.[4] It is likely that Thomas and Frances were of this family of Knottes.

During their marriage, Frances bore Richard eight children, William, the eldest, born in 1525[iii] and the first merchant adventurer of the family. He was followed by Richard, Humfrey, Thomas (1530–1576), and Edward, the youngest son, born about 1538, plus three daughters Joan, Elizabeth and Margaret. Edward and his mother inherited the land at Claverley and land at Hopton. The fourth son, Thomas Whitmore, who died in 1576 settled at nearby Ludstone and became the founder of the Ludstone branch of the

---

[3] Genealogy of the Billingsley family:
https://www.genealogy.com/ftm/p/o/t/Luke-W-Potter/index.html

[4] National Archives: Claverley Account Roll.

Ludstone Hall, Ludstone, Shropshire
Courtesy of John M / Ludstone Hall / CC BY-SA 2.0

family. He had two sons, John and William, and a daughter, Joyce, with his second wife Agnes Bowdler. Amid a formal garden of parterres, his son John rebuilt the original timber castle of Ludstone into a moated, castellated mansion named Ludstone Hall in 1607. Legend tells of a secret tunnel used by the monks at Ludstone to enter Claverley church at the time of the dissolution of the monasteries.

The Whitmores of Ludstone lived there for around four generations until it passed to the descendants of merchant adventurer William Whitmore. They held it for a further 250 years. Many of the Claverley and Ludstone Whitmores, their forebears and descendants, are buried at Claverley church, though the centuries of wind and rain have rendered the sandstone tombstones illegible.

What is known of Richard seems to indicate a forward-looking man of ability, a steely character doing whatever was needed to protect and enhance his property but one who other people trusted – a leader of men within his community, characteristics that his son William evidently inherited.

Beside his own manorial role, Richard acted as juror in 1520, and bailiff in 1521 and again in the years 1531 and 1538.[5] The bailiff was responsible for managing the manor, assigning jobs to the peasants, maintaining the local administration of justice at the manor court and helping the deserving poor. Medieval jurors were chosen as jurors because either they knew the parties and the facts or, if not, they had the responsibility to discover them. Jurors remained free to investigate cases on their own until the seventeenth century. Elected to the job as constable in 1548, Richard became responsible for keeping the peace, catching offenders, reporting to the court and enforcing the Tudor

---

[5] *Discovering Shropshire's History.*

punishments of ducking, whipping and the stocks. It was not a popular job. Sometimes, a well-to-do constable paid others to carry out such duties, thereby avoiding the friction that might arise with fellow citizens. In the same year, Richard is recorded as stopping the watercourse at Aston and Heathton but to what purpose has not been determined. Flooding from the River Severn can be a problem in Shropshire, and these villages lie close to the flood plain of Clun, so perhaps Richard was attempting a form of flood protection, or making sure his fields did not become arid in a dry summer.

Farming in Shropshire was a cooperative open field system whereby each manor or village had two or three large fields of several hundred acres each divided into many narrow strips of land cultivated by peasant families, often called tenants or serfs. However, by Richard's time this system was diminishing in favour of land enlosure for the rearing of sheep for meat as well as wool, but it was a system that deprived peasants of grazing pasture and caused them to leave their roots for the hope of betterment in the metropolis.

The markets of Europe had long desired the fine wool of Shropshire sheep, particularly those from around Shrewsbury and Bridgnorth. With the foundation in 1462 of the Shrewsbury Drapers Company and its staple in Oswestry, broadcloth, a dense woollen cloth finished and dyed in Flanders, also became an important commodity for export. The Company of Merchant Adventurers of London facilitated and protected the sale of these wares and the importation of wine and other commodities through its operation as a guild. Shropshire, therefore, had strong trading links not only within the county, but also with London and Europe.

As a result, Shrewsbury and the River Severn had become an important conduit for shipping all these commodities to London and thence to the European staple in Antwerp, which had an exclusive right to buy and sell. Because wool was England's most important product, the crown required all wool for export to be traded at a designated market, called the 'staple.' This allowed the crown to monitor the wool trade and levy tax on exports to Antwerp. There were also staples in Calais, Bruges, Middelburg and Stade for other items. Besides trade in wool something else was occurring. The wealthy in England and elsewhere were developing a love of luxury items, and as the Tudor age progressed such desires became more pronounced.

Perhaps, Richard foresaw that with changing tastes and expectation, London, the centre of English imports and exports, would be the place to make a fortune and apprenticed his eldest son there. William proved worthy of his father's faith in him and he did just that. By importing fine fabric from Spain as well as other goods, he rose to a prominent position with the City, master of the Haberdashers' Company and became one of the richest merchants of the sixteenth century.

William Whitmore 1525–1593

Apley Hall, nineteenth century, Geoff Cryer

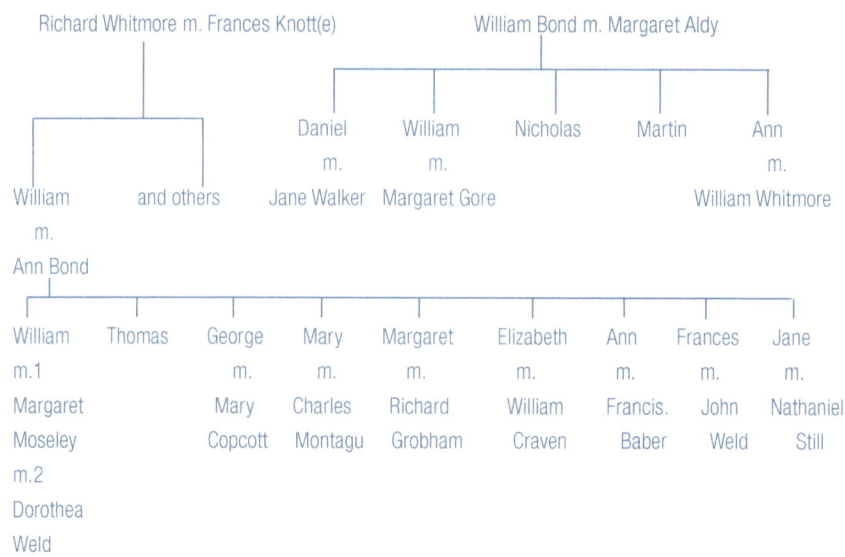

Events during his life time

- 1450–1648 Northern Renaissance
- 1533 Ann Boleyn married Henry VIII
- 1535–40 Dissolution of the Monasteries
- 1537 Hans Holbein became painter to King Henry VIII
- 1547 Start of reign of Edward VI
- 1553 Start of reign of Mary I

- 1558 Start of reign of Elizabeth I
- 1587 Mary, Queen of Scots executed
- 1588 Spanish Armada
- 1592–93 Plague in London reported by John Stow

William Whitmore's life spanned several major historical events: the destruction of the monasteries; the reformation; the accessions of Edward VI, Queen Mary I and Queen Elizabeth I; the executions of Lady Jane Grey, Ann Boleyn and Mary, Queen of Scots, and the Spanish Armada, with which he had some involvement.

Living at the same time as William were Machiavelli, the notorious Florentine statesman, and Paracelsus born in 1528, the writer of the first manual of surgery. Viewed as a portent of doom, the re-appearance of Halley's Comet in 1531 caused consternation. Some years later in 1550, chocolate arrived in England, thereafter the nation's favourite indulgence, and on 29 April 1553 a Flemish woman introduced the practice of starching linen to England. The Spanish Riding School in Vienna, with its famous white Lipizzaner stallions, whose elegant performances we still enjoy today, began operating in 1568.

William was born in the village of Claverley in 1525, the year Henry VIII began to seek annulment of his marriage to Katherine of Aragon. That single act had enormous consequences. It set England on a course that would affect William Whitmore and his fellow adventurers' future and adventuring activities, the safety of England's subjects and each Protestant monarch, especially Queen Elizabeth I. Henry VIII's separation from Rome set the scene for the divisive religious repercussions that would resonate throughout the reigns of the next six monarchs, repercussions which would draw William Whitmore, and indeed all England, into the ensuing religious and political maelstrom of the mid-sixteenth and seventeenth centuries.

Through separation from Rome, King Henry VIII began the process that led to English Protestantism and the English Reformation. King Henry's desire for a male heir became the drive that fuelled his passion for Ann Boleyn, referred to by her enemies as 'the Protestant Strumpet'. Hitherto England had been an adherent of the Roman Catholic Church of Rome but when Henry failed to persuade the pope to annul his marriage to his Spanish queen, he split from Rome and, with the use of propaganda in 'The Glass' and 'Articles of Council', he aimed to persuade the public to his reformation.

Monasteries, now no longer the strongholds of the Roman Catholic faith, had no purpose. Thomas Cromwell and priest Dr John London took control of the Dissolution of the Monasteries and sold off their rich tithed lands to fill the coffers of King Henry's treasury. Acting with the fervour of a zealot, Dr John London smashed shrines, desecrated religious sites, enriching himself and Cromwell in the process. Dr London was not a pleasant man; a bully, obsequious and cunning in the furtherance of his own ends, he was someone whose faith flowed with the tide of opinion and his own advantage. He was as severe against non-Anglican Protestants as he was against Roman Catholics. In 1520 he had been an adherent of the pope and chastised his nephew, Edward Planckney, for his evangelical views. Edward was a student at New College, Oxford where Dr John London was then a warden. For all his pious principles, they did not prevent him from being caught by his other nephew, Henry Planckney, in flagrante with two women, nor for his corruption of nuns at Chepstow in Wales. Caught out by his ungodly practises, in a fitting punishment of humiliation, he was made to ride through the streets facing the horse's tail to imprisonment in the Fleet prison where he died.

Some who sought to acquire the spoils of monastery lands had been the original donors of the land to the monasteries in the first place. In the years to come some of these properties would be acquired by the Whitmore family and their kin. Although his future actions were far from exemplary, King Henry never ceased to be a Catholic. He was a devout follower of the Catholic ritual and declared himself head of the Anglican Catholic Church of England free of interference from the popes, hence the English Reformation.

Richard Whitmore's will, with its reference to the Virgin Mary, might suggest that the Whitmore family church followed the Anglo-Catholic ritual at that time. But as King Edward, a Protestant, and his two sisters became queen, one a Catholic and the other a Protestant, in order to survive

Thirteenth-century frescoes at All Saints, Claverley

unhindered the Whitmore family must have accepted whichever creed was thrust upon them. Their local churches in Bobbington and Claverley were in the Royal Peculiar of the Deanery of Bridgnorth and fell directly under the jurisdiction of the British monarch rather than the bishops. In the shires, pragmatism was more important than dogma as people sought to go about their business undisturbed.

By 1902 the seventh-century All Saints at Claverley, which came into the patronage of the Whitmore family at a later date, was in need of repair. Eroded through the passage of time, the soft sandstone structure of this ancient church required restoration. As workmen stripped back the old plaster, painted murals were revealed. To everyone's astonishment, they were part of a thirteenth-century Bayeux-like fresco of fighting knights in armour, the only one of its kind in an English church; a rare find and now internationally famous.

The actions of Henry VIII may have begun the religious change but he was not solely responsible. Dissatisfaction with the teaching of the Church was already rife in Europe. Martin Luther, a German professor of theology who rejected the teaching of the Roman Catholic Church, had developed his own brand of Protestantism in Europe and it was gaining ground in England through the printing presses. This paved the way for the polarisation of Catholics and Protestants across much of Europe. From a political and personal point of view, many Englishmen preferred not to answer to Rome and those who had acquired monastery lands would naturally be unwilling to surrender them at a future date. It was not in their interest for the Roman Church to regain ascendency. Catholicism, once the dominant faith, now became a minority, but Protestantism set England on a course of conflict with the Roman Catholic countries of Europe, in particular the mighty Spanish and French. Both countries endeavoured for many years to put a Catholic on the throne of England; the Spanish through marriage and battle , the French by seeking to replace Elizabeth I with Mary, Queen of Scots, daughter of the French Mary of Guise, thereby furthering their 'auld alliance' with Scotland. These actions would affect the merchant adventurers of the Whitmore family, their Bond cousins and other kin for decades.

Change may wreak strife but history tells us that all great upheavals herald opportunities, sometimes for the better, in this case a renaissance and enlightenment, releasing a general vigour. Religion was an issue but in other spheres things were going well for England. By 1539 the wool and manufacturing trades were booming, leading to other changes. These trades demanded skills and training and that led individuals and the Guilds of Merchant Companies – mercers, drapers, grocers, haberdashers and goldsmiths – to found and endow schools. Schools of limited education had always existed, as had universities, Peterhouse College, Cambridge, founded in 1284, being the first, but those of the guilds aimed to educate boys as future mayors, merchants, royal ministers, clerks and lawyers. Such an education enabled them to govern the City and counties for the monarch and maintain well-run agricultural estates to provide food for the nation. The sons of yeomen, gentry and younger sons of the nobility and royalty joined the guilds and some of these became more successful than their elder brothers, who had to live off the proceeds of their inheritance and estates, many of which were burdened with debt.

Apprenticeship

At fourteen, William Whitmore, was old enough to become indentured with a master of the Company of Haberdashers'. Founded in mediaeval times, this livery company ranked amongst the 'Great Twelve City Livery Companies', each of which supported the work of the lord mayor, the City of London Corporation and the sheriffs of London. They also provided philanthropic fellowship, charity, professional education and safeguard for the members of their company. Whereas the wool and cloth merchants belonged to the Company of Drapers, the haberdashers were clothiers in ribbons, beads, sewn and fine materials, in particular silk and velvet. The name of William's master is not known. It has been suggested that Sir Francis Jones of Ludstone, his cousin, also a haberdasher, was his master. This cannot be the case since Francis, born around 1559, was thirty-four years younger than William.[6] William Jones, who established Monmouth Haberdashers' School, would not have been old enough either. It is likely, however, that William was placed with someone known to his family: a relation, or acquaintance, other than his father, which was prohibited. The father of Francis Jones of Ludstone was a haberdasher. Perhaps it was he who became William's master.

Besides regulating the cloth merchants' trade of exported cloth and imported silks and spices, the company also acted as an educational institute. Using the financial support offered by its merchants, it founded eight schools such as the Haberdashers' Aske's schools. In addition, several merchants started their own schools during the sixteenth century. Two such merchants were William Craven of the Merchant Taylors' Company, who

---

[6] Francis Jones became lord mayor of London in 1620. Francis died in 1623. See 'Parishes: Welford', A History of the County of Berkshire: Volume 4 (1924), pp. 116–125. URL:
http://www.british-history.ac.uk/report.aspx?compid=62691&strquery=Claverley

married William Whitmore's third daughter, Elizabeth; he founded Burnsall School in Yorkshire, and Whitmore's great friend Peter Blundell founded Tiverton School in Devon, now known as Blundell's School. At a later date, William Whitmore's brother-in-law, the haberdasher Martin Bond contributed towards the Haberdashers' Monmouth Schools. George Daniell, a businessman of Cornwall and grandson of Richard Daniell of this history endowed the still-existing Madron school in Cornwall for the education of sixty poor boys and girls in 1710.

There is very little information about William during his apprenticeship years because few apprenticeship records of that time now exist. Nevertheless, it is possible to gain an insight and general understanding of apprenticeships and the life that William lived at that time. Later in this history, we can also gain an appreciation of the livery companies and their relationship with the City of London, the difficulties encountered during trade and what effect they had on William.

Obtaining an apprenticeship was no easy matter. Apprentices had to qualify for admittance and the guilds with the highest status expected the best qualifications. They were also the most expensive to join. Apprentices not only had to be literate, they had to be legitimate, born in Britain, without disability and aged between fourteen and sixteen years of age. To finance his son's apprenticeship and living expenses William's father paid a bond to the apprentice master with whom William lived; a not too onerous expense for Richard. Claverley was amongst the richer agricultural areas of Shropshire and the landed Richard, affluent enough to provide endowments to the poor of the parish and loans to friends, must have considered the expense worthwhile.

Training to become a master within a prestigious guild provided a valuable network of future contacts and profitable employment. The friendships and marriages forged within the guilds gave stability to family and business and were the means whereby families could nourish their fortunes and social status; a fact borne out by many of the people who became Whitmore relations and descendants. Through this network of associations, it becomes apparent that eventually nearly everyone became related to everyone else.[7 8,]

Throughout history, the high spirits of the young has sometimes spiralled into bad behaviour and drunken brawls. Even Pompeii had its problems. A

---

[7] *The Early Tudors: England 1485–1558* by David Hudson, David Rogerson, and Samantha Ellsmore. Published by Hodder Education, 2001. Also The Reign of Elizabeth 1558–160 by J.B. Black.

[8] *The Internal Organisation of the Merchant Adventurers of England* by W.E. Lingelbach. Published online by Cambridge University Press: 12 February 2009. See Transactions of the Royal Historical Society.

wall discovered in the ruins of Pompei begs the question, '*What can we do about the young?*' William's era was no exception but England's renaissance elders had a fair idea how to solve the problem. Apprenticeships! They considered a seven-year training, whether merited or not, a worthy solution to the tricky question of how to occupy intelligent adolescent boys and sometimes girls. It kept them off the streets, usefully employed and provided them with the purpose and skills for future employment. Wild behaviour was not an option for those who wished to succeed. Retribution soon followed for the wayward who broke the rules and obligations of the guild, not only for the apprentice, but also for his master for not demanding better conduct. In this way, the exuberance of youth was kept under reasonable control.

Thus, the rules of apprenticeships obliged William's master to provide him with a good training, discipline, and an understanding of the complex social graces expected of a businessman in Tudor England. Failure to fulfil this responsibility incurred a severe fine and the removal of the apprentice to another master. For his part, William, still a child, had to obey the rules of his master's household. Like all apprentices, he was prohibited from entering ale-houses and taverns and he could not go out without first seeking permission from his master and stating where and with whom he was going.

Tudor and Stuart society abided by a rigorous code of etiquette and courtesy, which involved an elaborate protocol of respect. The Tudors placed high regard on presentation. For them, ceremony and etiquette related to all aspects of life and on such knowledge rested the success of the chosen career. Successful apprentices had an expectation of becoming leaders of commerce and their guild with the prospect of holding positions of authority within the ruling hierarchy of the City. The best and wealthiest of them would become lord mayor of London. Such a role conferred a status equivalent to that of an earl with power second only to the monarch. Such posts involved a good knowledge of the very complex duties associated with business and ceremony.

Those expecting service from servants in the future had first to learn how to serve, and Sunday was the time to practice the twin arts of service and courtesy. In so doing, William would be expected to wait on his apprentice master and mistress at church and serve them lunch and supper. No matter how wealthy or grand the background of the apprentice, respect and good manners forbade ostentation or the wearing of apparel grander than that of the master. These were lessons well learnt by William. His adult life and his will reveal a man of culture and kindness, a gift for friendship as well as acute business sense. His friends, family and servants were cared for and his children, still young, at the time of his death bidden to '*love one another and respect and obey their mother.*'

Despite such meticulous regulation, many apprentices failed to complete their training, and others did not get beyond the journeyman stage in their career. This was not necessarily through lack of ability and application but often through lack of money. Wealthy merchants tried to address that problem by bequeathing sums of money and gifts to charities that supported struggling apprentices. William did likewise. He bequeathed 40 shillings (about £340 today) to be paid to Roger Harrison, a Smith, for the upbringing of William Naylor.[9] Around that time a labourer could make about a shilling a day, a shop apprentice about 6 pence a day, a merchant £100 p.a. and a very successful merchant, such as William, £100,000 p.a., the equivalent of £17,000,000 at today's prices (2017). Compared with William's wealth £340 may seem a small sum but he also supported other causes. At the time of his death, he had a wife and nine young children whose welfare he had to protect through the many years to come by providing them with money for widowhood, the dowries expected of a good marriage or annuities if unmarried.

Although twenty-one is the usual age of adulthood, the livery companies did not consider young people sufficiently mature for marriage until the age of twenty-four, a fact supported by science today. Scientists have concluded that the brain is not fully mature until after the age of twenty-one. A considerable number of men, including William, were a great deal older than that when they married. No respectable father of high social status would permit his daughter to marry a husband without means and prospects. A suitor had to have already consolidated his career and standing within the community or have expectation of inherited wealth and title. William did not marry until he was forty-seven. Unfortunately, a late marriage meant that many children were young when their father died, making their future dependent upon their father's past success and their mother's social talents.

The haberdasher's motto is 'Serve and Obey' and William fulfilled this promise. He became a freeman of his livery company and a freeman of the City of London. By the end of his life, he had become one of the richest of the City merchants and the owner of a great estate. The livery companies and their guilds enrobed the most able and financially secure merchants as members; William was both, and entitled to wear the blue and white clothing of the haberdashers. Most liverymen progressed through the hierarchy to become members of their company's court and in due course the master of the company for a year, as did William.

Membership provided rewards but it was not without expense and civic

---

[9] Tudor Hackney: Local government and the Poor
https://www.nationalarchives.gov.uk/education/tudorhackney/localhistory/lochlg.asp

responsibility. This was the age of pageantry and it played a significant part in people's lives, giving dignity to occasions as well as entertainment to the populace. Civic ceremonies such as mayoral processions or the entry of royalty into the City were generally the preserve of these elite groups. It was obligatory to attend feasts, memorial masses and processions; failure to appear incurred fines. All this required finery, and guild members had to purchase the appropriate ceremonial livery gown and hood, sometimes annually, if the design and colour changed, or the occasion merited further grandeur.

It was to William's credit that he had done so well. It was much harder to succeed in the large metropolis that London had now become than in a provincial town. From the time of William's birth to the end of his life the inhabitants of London had risen from 60,000 to 200,000 as people from the shires, and immigrants fleeing from disruption or persecution elsewhere, flooded into the City. Not only was the merchant trade to which he belonged highly competitive, especially with immigrants eager for work, it endured years of disruption caused by political turbulence, battles and foreign domination.[10]

The Great Companies' entrepreneurial spirit and the financial independence of their members fostered private enterprise, self-government and self-reliance making these companies more or less independent of the state. This oligarchy of senior London merchants governed the City of London as its aldermen, sheriffs and lord mayors, and their status allowed them to use their impressive resources to pursue their aims, politically and administratively. They contributed to the welfare of the City through payment of quarterly alms, provided levies for civil projects and the funds for building developments such as halls, chapels and alms-houses. They represented the interests and aspirations of those who were not members so long as they did not threaten the guilds' merchandising. They engaged in trade across Europe and the merchant adventurers amongst them funded the discovery of other shores revealing the questing character of the nation's Saxon, Viking and Norman heritage. It was this spirit of adventure that fuelled Britain's future dominance in the world; the establishment of her colonies, Commonwealth and Empire to become Great Britain.

The aldermanry's wealth, their commercial and political knowledge at home and abroad and their links with Parliament enabled a close and valuable relationship with the monarch. Loans by their company to the crown and the personal loans provided by affluent members gave them the power to exercise some political influence. This would sometimes be in their

---

[10] *A Companion to Tudor Britain* by Robert Tittler, Norman Leslie Jones.

own interests, but then, to some degree, it was their enterprise and money that enabled England to gain supremacy and prosperity. These companies became the force that helped drive social and political change. The wealth of the nation now included the merchant class as well as the nobility; a valuable resource and one of lively ingenuity.

The Merchant Years

Although described as an elite merchant of Spain, the available details of William's trading activities are not numerous but they suggest a highly successful, personable businessman with a variety of contacts across the City and court as shown by his will and the marriages of his offspring. Whereas there is a fair amount of information about some of his relations' activities as merchant adventurers during the same period, this lack of information for William Whitmore may point to a more reserved and independent individual. Or it may indicate that he spent much of his early life conducting business overseas. There is, however, some evidence that he had some sort of partnership with the merchant tailors, William Parker, Peter Blundell and Sir William Craven, who became lord mayor of London. Their wills certainly indicate great friendship. William Craven traded in England rather than abroad and William Whitmore, a merchant adventurer of fine silks and cloth from Spain, is likely to have sold his rich fabrics in England through Craven and Craven's newly established warehouses. Around £600 worth (£60,000 today) of William Craven's material draped Queen Elizabeth's funeral cortège. Could this have been acquired through William Whitmore or his sons? Possibly.

As his merchandising activities increased in future years, besides travelling overseas himself, William engaged others to work on his behalf and indeed among the bequests in his will were his clerks and agents, Henry Polstead (Polstede) and John Bladwell. John Bladwell may have acted as William's agent overseas.[11] A successful merchant worked very hard not only on the bartering side of the business but also on the onerous task of maintaining accounting ledgers, details of purchases, sales and payments and he would also be well acquainted with the laws and ordinances of the merchant adventurers of England.[12] These tasks together with business correspondence in Britain and abroad, all had to be kept in meticulous

---

[11] John Bladwell's children were naturalised in 1610, indicating that they were born overseas while their father worked as William Whitmores agent.

[12] The Merchant Adventurers of England, their laws and ordinances with other documents by William E Lingelbach (William Ezra), 1871–1962.

detailed order if a merchant were to remain solvent. William sealed the hand-written business transactions, accounts and letters with his personal seal, which may have been a falcon as used by his thirteenth-century ancestor John de Whytmere. The falcon is also depicted on the crest of the Whitmore coat of arms. Several copies of transactions were made in case of loss, each to be held in a letter book. These were the tasks with which Henry Polstede would have helped. At home, family and friendships had to be maintained.

Having completed his apprenticeship at twenty-four years of age, William embarked upon his trading activities. Henry VIII had died and Edward VI was now king, but not all was well back home in Shropshire. William's father at fifty-four, not particularly old by Whitmore standards of that era, was either ailing or badly injured. On 22 August 1549 he wrote his will and three weeks later he was dead. With only herbal medicine and other concoctions to help, many died of what we today would consider minor ailments.

Richard's will demonstrates his care and forethought for his family. It stipulates William's responsibility towards his mother Frances and his younger brothers and sisters. It is interesting to note that William was to receive his inheritance at the age of thirty unless the executrix thought otherwise, yet his brothers and sisters would receive theirs at twenty-one; a wise and thoughtful move on the part of Richard Whitmore. He thereby ensured that his heir took responsibility for the fatherless family and their welfare. By the time William was thirty his brothers and sisters would have reached adulthood. A further condition of the will was that William pay rent for his father's lands during the lifetimes of his mother and brothers, providing them with an income and continuance in the family home. It is an indication that William now had an adequate income of his own. If William did not agree to this he was to receive the much smaller child's portion of his inheritance, which would be the same sum as his father's bequest to the poor of the parish of Claverley and less than his brothers and sisters. The will was proved at Bridgnorth on the 12 September 1549 (3^d Edw. VI).[13]

In Tudor times it was customary for the eldest, which was William, to inherit the estate, while the younger brothers would be sent into trade, law or politics. Unusually, under the will of his father, the youngest brother, Edward, born in 1538 and eleven years old when his father died, inherited land held at Claverley and Hopton, rather than his older brothers, presumably to ensure his welfare during childhood. The other brothers were approaching their adult and earning years and William had his own resources. These lands eventually came to William or his descendants, so Edward had probably died

---

[13] *Whitmore Notes and Tracts* by W. H. Whitmore.

sometime before 1593. Brother Thomas held land in nearby Ludstone, and made his own fortune, possibly through trade and property speculation. It is not known what happened to Richard and Humphrey or his sisters other than Joan. Their mother, Frances, went on to marry William Barker of Aston and produced three more sons, Francis, John and William Barker Jr, and two daughters. William Whitmore was evidently on good terms with these half-brothers, who are mentioned in his will. Since William's will mentions only sister Joan but none of his brothers by his father, it would appear that they had probably predeceased him or had sufficient resources of their own. We know from the chapter on John Johnson that the sweating sickness occurred in 1551 and it is recorded that its occurrence in Shrewsbury led people to flee to the surrounding villages taking the disease with them. It is feasible that William's brothers had become its victims.

For his mother to have had a second family she must have been in her teens when she married Richard Whitmore. She died thirty-four years after Richard in 1583. Her second husband, William Barker, died in 1590.[14]

Trading in Spain

Spanish Company Arms[15]

After his father's death William returned to his City premises in Lombard Street, situated within the financial and mercantile heart of London where the merchants carried out their transactions. While their counterparts in the ancient city of Antwerp had the benefit of the magnificent bourse, the merchants of London conducted the business of negotiating loans, conveying international news, calculating rates of exchange and all the other aspects of international trade outdoors on Lombard Street regardless of the extremes of the English climate. That continued until 1576 when Thomas Gresham founded the Royal Exchange.

William also acquired the Balmes estate (sometimes referred to as Baume), rented from the Philpot family. Balmes House and its farm lay within the village of Hackney,[16] in what was then the pastoral area of Hoxton, lying north of Regent's Canal, and just outside the northeast city wall; a suitable residence in which a well-to-do merchant could relax and entertain. William's eldest son, Sir William Whitmore, later bought this estate in 1634 for his younger brother,

---

[14] Claverley Parish Registers http://www.melocki.org.uk/salop/Claverley.html .
[15] Wikipedia.
[16] Tudor Hackney.The National Archives.
https://www.nationalarchives.gov.uk/education/resources/tudor-hackney/

Sir George Whitmore, whose son and grandson inherited it. On the death of the grandson it reverted to William's descendants at Apley Park, Shropshire and was then sold by their cousin, Lord Craven.

On warm summer evenings people would stroll across the surrounding meadows of Balmes and Hackney village, enjoying the sweet scent of grass and hedgerows as described a century later by Samuel Pepys.[17] Though close to William's City residence, Balmes must have afforded a pleasant retreat from the detritus of London's citizens and hubbub of street vendors in the mushrooming City.

Besides his merchandising activities, William had also to find time to train his apprentices, which would not have included his own sons since the rules of the livery companies forbade that. Nevertheless, sons William and George became members of the Haberdasher Company but through patrimony rather than apprenticeship.

The majority of William Whitmore's trading activities coincided with the reign of Elizabeth I. What was it about this era that drove William's merchandising choices and ultimate success? *The Travels of Marco Polo* published around 1300, plus tales of splendour and exotic wares from faraway places had, over time, helped to change tastes and expectations. The Tudors took pleasure in the arts, sporting events and ceremonial extravaganza. Well-to-do Elizabethans enjoyed the art of Nicholas Hilliard and Hans Holbein, the music of William Byrd and Thomas Tallis while the plays and poetry of Shakespeare and Edmund Spenser filled the theatre. Such entertainments and pageantry required appropriate dress, while better housing required furnishing fabrics to match their owners aspirations. However impoverished the English treasury may have been compared with that of Spain and France, the successful echelons of society grew richer and so too did their desire for spices, tapestries and fine, jewel-encrusted fabric with which to adorn their person and stately homes. Originally, the wealthy and rich merchants preferred to have their clothes made by the skilled workers of Antwerp and that continued until Antwerp's artisans fled from Spanish hostility to find refuge in London. It was this desire for silks and fine cloth that caught the attention of William, the haberdasher.

As the emphasis on imports increased the astute William became a merchant adventurer of London. This was a title originally given to merchants in England engaged mainly in the export of wool and undyed broadcloth,[18] their profits enabling import of foreign goods, as already described. Later, it came to mean those engaged in exports and willing to

---

[17] Pepys Diaries.
[18] A dense woollen cloth.

risk their money in speculative ventures. As merchant adventurers instead of sole traders, they belonged to a powerful, regulated company in the nature of a guild. The problems encountered made it increasingly clear that the merchants needed the protection of incorporation. Politics and the religious problems of the Lowland countries presented difficulties for the English wool staple, leading to a decline in the export of wool, making it necessary to trade further afield. The European recession between 1530–1570 also meant that the wool industry and its workers at home needed protection, thus the government passed a law in 1570 requiring all Englishmen except nobles to wear a woollen cap to church on Sunday.

This European recession persuaded William and fellow merchants to trade with Spain as members of the first Spanish Company founded 1530–1585.[19] William succeeded in his mission against considerable inconveniencies, because if trade in Northern Europe suffered intermittent disruption through religious strife and political hostility it became equally difficult with Spain because of deteriorating Anglo–Spanish relations, European recession and the recession of Seville business, which affected the Spanish economy. In England, as John Johnson found, credit collapsed because the English monetary system had become debased through debt incurred by Henry VIII. English trade worsened in the 1560s when Spain placed a temporary embargo on English goods on account of English privateers making a nuisance of themselves around Spanish ports.

Around the same time, England infuriated the Portuguese by intruding into her African territory. The Portuguese responded by closing their ports to English traders until 1576. Yet, as always, there are those who defy defeat, no matter what difficulties are imposed. Intrepid and innovative merchants found loopholes and engaged in illicit trading.

These problems made it necessary to have a more formal trading arrangement and after protracted negotiation, Spanish trade was formalised via a Chartered Spanish and Portuguese Company in 1577. The membership consisted of over 200 London merchants, including William Whitmore, and 173 merchants from other ports. The business of commerce took place in the Andalusian ports of Seville, San Lucar de Barrameda, Puerto de Santa Maria and Cadiz. Company members traded using their own capital, subject to the common rules of the corporation.

Throughout twenty years of mercantile business William Whitmore had negotiated his way through several setbacks and had accumulated significant

---

[19] 'Introduction: The first Spanish company, 1530–85', in *The Spanish Company*, ed. Pauline Croft (London, 1973), pp. vii–xxix. *British History Online* http://www.british-history.ac.uk/london-record-soc/vol9/vii-xxix [accessed 4 February 2021].

resources. Other prosperous merchants and courtiers were building magnificent mansions for themselves. Sir Christopher Hatton built Holdenby and owned the even grander Kirby Hall, where William's granddaughter would one day live.[20] Likewise, in 1572 William purchased the Apley Park estate in Shropshire from Sir Thomas Lucy, while also retaining the Balmes estate on the outskirt of London and his work-based City residence in Lombard Street. Fortunately, the rules relating to trading in London while holding a rural estate had changed around 1545. Until then, a merchant with a property outside London could fall between two opposing forces jealous of his success. In London, a merchant's Freedom of the City could be revoked because of his country property, yet traders in the county of his estate cited his Freedom of the City. The impasse could result in the hapless merchant paying fines and taxes in both City and county.

The Apley Hall of William's time was a large, mediaeval edifice surrounded by parkland overlooking the reaches of the River Severn. Apley, an Anglo-Saxon name meaning 'a clearing in the forest where apples grow', in other words an orchard, was to be the home of each heir for over three hundred years until they moved to other estates in England.

The old building was replaced in the 1600s by a large, imposing mansion with formal terracing. The walled area contained several other buildings, which may have been the dairy, a fish house, grain store and other offices usual at that time.[21] In the nineteenth century, a descendant rebuilt the hall as an imposing, castellated, stately mansion described by one inhabitant as an *'earthly paradise for children'*. Indeed, PG Wodehouse, who had lived in Shropshire during his childhood, used Apley as the inspiration for Blandings Castle in his Jeeves novels. Much more surprising, Operation Sealion, 1941, outlining Hitler's plans after his invasion of England, had been found by a soldier at a deserted Nazi post in Belgium in 1945.[22] To the amazement of the British establishment, these papers show that Hitler thought the nearby town of Bridgnorth the ideal place for his Nazi headquarters once he had

---

[20] The home of William's granddaughter Elizabeth when she married the 1st Lord Christopher Hatton from the Hattons of Hatton, Cheshire, a relation of the first Sir Christopher Hatton.

[21] Shropshire Deer Parks: Recreation, Status and Husbandry. PhD Thesis by Sandra Morris, School of History, University of East Anglia Feb. 2015. This states that Apley Hall was demolished in the English Civil War but is not thought to have taken place.

[22] Unverified papers discovered refer to Operation Sealion detailing the German plans for invading Britain. Bridgnorth was mentioned and thought to indicate Hitler's intention to base his headquarters there owing to its strategically central position.

conquered Britain! Apley Park was his intended home. That Hitler should choose the small, rural town of Bridgnorth as a Nazi headquarters rather than some other larger city is intriguing, but it is well positioned for maintaining contact with other regions. That he should choose the stately and renovated Apley as his home is perhaps less remarkable since no expense had been spared in its rebuilding but one wonders how he knew about it. Hitler's intentions towards the British as described in these papers are very chilling.

The year 1572 was a momentous year for William; not only did he acquire Apley Park, he also married a girl around half his forty-seven years of age. She was Ann Bond, born some time between 1549 and 1553[iv] the young widow of merchant Robert King, and daughter of fellow merchant adventurer, William Bond and his wife Margaret Aldy of Guildford, Surrey. Ann was the niece of Sir George Bond, lord mayor of London 1587–88 during the Spanish Armada, and sister of Captain Martin Bond MP whose story will be told in a later chapter.

William Whitmore and Ann Bond[23]

William and Ann had nine children, three sons, William b. 1573, Thomas b. 1574 and George b. probably around 1576 and six daughters, Margaret b. ca. 1574, Ann b. 1582, Elizabeth, their third daughter, Mary, Frances b. ca. 1586 and the youngest, Jane. The parish records for Claverley, dating from 1568, do not record their births, yet their cousins at Ludstone Hall are all mentioned. Nor is there any mention of them at St. John's church, which served the Balmes estate in the vicinity of Hackney. They are, therefore, likely to have been christened at St. Edmund, King and Martyr in Lombard Street, London. Unfortunately, the registers for St. Edmund were burnt in the Great Fire of London and do not start again until 1670 after it was rebuilt.

---

[23] Pictures of William Whitmore and his wife – part of a lantern slide collection.

The dates of birth have probably been calculated from other events and documents but they fit with other known facts.

With business activities based in the City, the family continued to live in London between the Lombard Street and the Balmes residences, rather than the Apley estate, which may have been used for farming, now increasingly important for feeding the nation. London was also a better base for maintaining contacts with merchant friends and possibly the schooling of the children. William's sons are not mentioned in the registers of Bridgnorth School, which opened in 1505, or Shrewsbury in 1552, though it is possible that not all the records have survived. Alternatively, London had the famous Tudor school St. Anthony's close to their father's business premises in Lombard Street. Other schools in the vicinity were the Merchant Taylors School founded 1561, St Paul's founded in 1505 and Eton College 1440. Although later generations of the family are recorded at these schools, there appears to be no mention of William's children in the surviving records probably because they had private tutors. It is believed the eldest son, William, went up to King's College, Cambridge University, and then studied law at the Middle Temple. Son Thomas, died in his thirties during 1612. It is possible that he attended one of the inns of law and acted as an agent for the Apley estate. William set up his youngest son, George, as a merchant in the Netherlands where he was in partnership with Richard Daniell of this history.[24] William also had to make provision for the future of his six daughters; dowries if they married, or annuities if not. In Tudor England the nurture of contacts played an important role in finding suitable spouses for offspring. In fact, after his death, all William and Ann's daughters married into leading City, legal and ecclesiastic families.

After his marriage, William continued to trade with Spain even though Anglo–Spanish politics steadily worsened culminating in the launch of the Spanish Armada. Suspecting the Spanish king's intentions to invade, the English merchants had played their part in a variety of tactics aimed at delaying confrontation. William, with his wife's cousin Sir William Bond, contributed to delaying the start of the Armada by putting financial pressure on the pope and the Spanish king. For this a grateful Queen Elizabeth granted William Whitmore a second crest to his coat of arms.[25] The following chapters on the Bond relations and the Armada outline the adversities the merchants faced as the political situation escalated into battle, and what happened thereafter.

William's heyday in trade had gained him considerable financial resources

---

[24] Alexander Daniell's diary relates that George had some estate in the Netherlands in the early 1600s.
[25] Coat of Arms granted 1593 by Sir William Dethick, Garter King of Arms.

and in his later years he took on roles within the City. According to the rules of the City, freemen of the City had an obligation to become aldermen, if asked. William had already been a governor of Christ's Hospital for four years from 1581–1585 when on 9 January 1589 he was nominated to the aldermanry of the City of London. A refusal of the appointment broke the Freeman's Oath and was considered a serious offence; one that incurred harsh penalties as his nephew, Sir William Bond would later discover. By refusing the aldermanry of Farringdon Ward in 1605 Sir William Bond was thrown into Newgate prison until he changed his mind. William Whitmore would have been well aware of the risk but decided against the offer. Repercussions duly followed. He was discharged by the Common Council five days later and fined £200, ca. £25,000 in today's currency.[26] What could have happened to make this otherwise honourable man decline? Could it be his health? He had already relinquished his post as governor of Christ's Church. At sixty-four years of age he had done well to survive so long, especially as there had been serious outbreaks of the plague in the 1560s, or perhaps he was feeling his age. However, his future decisions seem not to bear this out. The haberdasher records list a Mr Whitmore as master of the company of Haberdashers in 1590 and 1591. This might have been William but could have been his brother, George.[27] Without further information it is not possible to know for sure. In 1592 William again took on the governorship of Christ's Hospital. The hospital had been founded to care for the honest and respectable poor, the disabled, the elderly, and orphans. It also educated and provided apprenticeships for the children in its care.

Perhaps William was suffering from intermittent health problems and felt the extra job of an alderman too onerous. It was certainly a demanding role. He knew he could afford the aldermanry penalties and perhaps he preferred to devote what remained of his life to his young family. There is, however, another possibility. William had to think ahead to the future of his family. Though extremely wealthy, the duties of an alderman incurred considerable

---

[26] The Aldermen of the City of London – Alfred P. Beaven *Sworn Jan. 9, 1589] [Nominated: William Whitmore (Haberdasher), R. Gourney, T. Lawrence]* Rep. 22, ff. 14, 17 b *Discharged by the Common Council, January 14, 1589; fine of £200 (Journal 22, fo. 252). From: 'Aldermen of the City of London: Portsoken ward', The Aldermen of the City of London: Temp. Henry III – 1912 (1908), pp. 179–188.* URL:
http://www.british-history.ac.uk/report.aspx?compid=67211&strquery Journal 22, fo. 252.

[27] Haberdasher Records for London 1526–1933: Haberdashers, Apprentices and Freemen https://search.findmypast.co.uk/results/world-records/city-of-london-haberdashers-apprentices-and-freemen-1526–1933?lastname=whitmore&_page=2

expense. Not only that, there was the very real prospect of being elected as lord mayor of London. That role was even more financially onerous as well as demanding. It became ruinous for his cousin Sir Francis Jones; his term as lord mayor of London led to crippling debt. It bankrupted some. Some aldermen preferred to forego the honour and liability. William perhaps intended to ensure his children's inheritance rather than pursue a prestigious position.

William died at the age of sixty-eight on 8 August 1593, why is not known, but towards the end of 1592 a major outbreak of the plague (Black Death) occurred, which lasted until December 1593. In London, the worst of it occurred during the summer months of 1593. Out of 150,000 people living within the City wall, around 11,000 died. However, all William's family survived and William was able to dictate his will on 6 August 1593. This implies that William had not succumbed to the pestilence, because it is unlikely that anyone would have been permitted to enter the house to help write his will.[28] William requested that he be buried at St. Edmund the Martyr, close to his business address at Lombard Street. Although nearly all the other merchants of this history are mentioned in the London Subsidy Rolls, William Whitmore is not listed. There may be several reasons for this. In the mid-1500s he may have been overseas. Other reasons include damage to part of the Rolls, his name missed, or not yet digitised or he was registered at his mansion in Shropshire, or his residence in Hackney, which may not have been included in the Rolls.

Among William's possessions were his residences in London and Shropshire and investments in property and manors in several counties. His will makes it clear that the family were on close terms with their Shropshire relatives including Williams's half-brothers, John, Francis and William Barker, to whom he left bequests. His full brothers are not mentioned, having probably predeceased him, but one of his sisters, Joan Lewis, and a cousin, Francis Jones, are cited.

It is said that the company a man keeps reveals his character. William moved in affluent but altruistic circles. His will provides insight into his generosity and thoughtfulness towards his family, his four menial house servants, Thomas, Robert, Katherine and Marjory, and two business servants, Henry Polstead (Polstede) and John Bladwell. Other beneficiaries included a past servant, Raf Bruskin, and his apprentice, William Okes. Close friends and fellow merchants John Gardener, Peter Blundell and Robert Bladwell were not forgotten. William and Ann had been genial

---

[28] *History of Epidemics in Britain*, by Charles Creighton, M.A., M.D. 1891. AAAIAAJ?hl=en&gbpv=1&dq=plague+1592&pg=PA351&printsec=frontcover#PPA352,M1.

hosts. Theirs had been a large home of comfort and some splendour, filled with friends, one or two of whom are thought to have lived with them from time-to-time, in particular William's clerk, Henry Polstede, and friend Peter Blundell.

It was customary on the death of the head of the family where there were children under twenty-one, to draw up an inventory of possessions and put sureties in the City Chambers for the money due to the children.[29] William's inventory for the Balmes estate was made on parchment 5½ inches across and over 49 feet long. Besides possessions, it included outstanding debts owing to William in England. Apley is not included, nor is the Lombard Street house, indicating that the Balmes residence was their main family home.

The Balmes estate consisted of a farm, formal gardens and a large house with many bedchambers, a nursery, widow's chamber, parlours and hall. Attached to it were the buttery, dairy, pastry house, fish house, kitchen and counting house and cellars. The family's possession of two virginals hints at an enjoyment of music. William's clothes, made of fine silk included doublets and coats. Amongst his armoury were corselets, gauntlets, headpieces, muskets, swords, daggers, long bows and arrows, clothes to cover the armour and quilted coats for horsemen. When and how these were used is not known. They point to an era when readiness to protect the City and family were important. Also, the arms and munition could indicate a swashbuckling past of hand-fighting and grappling on the high seas against pirates and foreign privateers during the early years of William's life. William did not marry until his late forties and apparently did not serve as either an alderman or sheriff in his earlier years. This suggests an absence overseas and this possibility is strengthened by the scarcity of information about his activities in those years.

William's heir, the later knighted Sir William Whitmore, had almost reached adulthood and he inherited Apley. William's wife Ann received the Balmes estate. Much of the rest was to be divided equally between the sons with provision for the daughters. Ann, his wife, was an accomplished investor herself and maintained the family's fortune by investing in yet more land. In 1613 King James granted her the manor of Keynsham. She raised the rents and made more money from the mills. This manor remained within the family as absentee landlords until the eighteenth century about 150 years later when it was sold to Edward Lyne MD.[30] Although the Whitmores invested agriculturally in their Shropshire manors, Keynsham had simply provided revenue from the rents. The people of Keynsham, therefore, managed the area for themselves with little interference from their landlord

---

[29] Abstracts of the inventory were recorded in the Common Sergeant's Book.
[30] *The History and Antiquities of the Counties of Somerset Volume 2* by John Collinson.

– good for those living in that era but unfortunate in the long term for later incumbents. With little agricultural investment and a surprising lack of foresight and prudence by the usually astute Whitmore landlords, Keynsham inevitably became less prosperous and, compared to better managed and improved areas, less of an asset.

The Balmes farm bequeathed to Ann eventually devolved to her youngest son, Sir George Whitmore. At her death over twenty years later, on 9 October 1615, Ann is recorded as living at the Lombard Street address, having probably moved there when son George married in 1611.[31] Ann and William Whitmore were buried alongside each other but sadly the flames of the Great Fire consumed all within its path and nothing remains of the mediaeval St. Edmund's. It was replaced by a new church built to the design of Sir Christopher Wren.

William and Ann had been benefactors of a number of causes in their lifetime as well as through their wills. Aware that the rising population created unemployment and poverty, the couple each gave to the hospitals of St. Thomas's, St. Bartholomew, Christ's, and Brideswell to provide work for the poor, Brideswell receiving £200 from William and Christ's £400 from his wife, Ann.[32]

Written on the wall on the west side of Brideswell Hospital is the following notation:

WILLIAM WHITMORE LATE CITIZEN THE HABBER of
LONDON GAVE TOWARDS SETTING POORE PEOPLE To
WORK IN THIS HOSPITALL 200 l MRS ANN WHITMORE
WIDOW OF THE SAID MR WHITMORE GAVE TO THE SAME
USE 150 l.
On a Table of the Benefactors in the Court Room
1600 Mr William Whitmore 200 l.
1615 Mrs Ann Whitmore 150 l.

William donated to Langborne Ward, and made provision for the relief of the unfortunate debtors who had fallen on hard times and were held within the Ludgate and Comptor Prisons.[33] The Haberdashers Company also received an interest-free loan of £400 for four young men of the Company of Merchant Adventurers, for four years.[34]

---

[31] Hackney Registers.

[32] Will of William Whitmore d. 1593. John Strype's Survey of the Cities of London and Westminster.

[33] A small prison run by a sheriff for civil prisoners – debtors and dissenters.

Over the years, the City had developed a system for the sale of sea-coals to the poor at cheap rates in winter. In addition, livery companies were obliged to lay up cheap stores of corn for sale during times of scarcity. Bearing in mind that the 1500s experienced a mini ice age, these were much needed resources for the poverty-stricken. After William's death, Ann continued to be conscious of their plight and in a codicil to her will of 21 January 1613 she bequeathed messuages, that is, land or houses, in Bishopsgate Street to the Haberdashers' Company. She intended that the company use the rents to buy coal for the poor of St. Edmund the King and Martyr, gowns for ten poor widows of freemen and to provide money for wardens of the company. The bequest was still fulfilling its aims in 1861 through the haberdashers' possession of no. 18 Bishopsgate Street.[35] Bishopsgate Street was originally a Roman road leading from London to Cambridge. Situated within the vicinity of the new tower named the 'Gherkin,' no. 18 may have been demolished. Ann also left bequests to several ministers: the erudite Ephraim Pagit, a Royalist and anti-Presbyterian minister of her local church St. Edmund the King and Martyr, Thomas Gataker, a Puritan divine and Whitmore kinsman who had been disinherited by his Catholic family for his Protestant (heretic) views, and Mr Spindlowe.[36] This spirit of altruism passed from parents to son, in particular the youngest son, Sir George, a future lord mayor of London, and his sons. These Whitmores were considered to be among the godly of London.

William's friend, Peter Blundell, a London merchant also of immense fortune, had no kin but found a surrogate family within the hospitality of William and Ann's home where he spent a considerable amount of time. In return for their friendship and hospitality, Ann, her nine children and all their servants, past and present, became beneficiaries of Peter Blundell's will in 1601.[37] Other recipients included Ann's brothers, Martin and William Bond, and William Whitmore's clerk, Henry Polstead (Polstede).

Peter Blundell provided benevolence to a very wide range of friends and causes and, in demonstration of his strong wish to ensure the success of others through education, he founded Blundell's School originally known as Tiverton School.

---

[34] The Endowed Charities of the City of London. Reprinted at Large from Seventeen Reports By Great Britain. Commissioners for Inquiring Concerning Charities.

[35] John Strype's Survey of the Cities of London and Westminster.

[36] *Local Identities in Late Medieval and Early Modern England* edited by N. Jones, D. Woolf : The Charity of London Widows pp. 198.

[37] *Donations of Peter Blundell (Founder) and Other Benefactors to The Free Grammar School at Tiverton* by Benjamin Incledon, Exeter: E. Grigg, typ. (1792).

' ... though I am not myself a scholar, I will be the means of making more scholars than anyone else in England.'

Almost a century later in 1694, Sir William Whitmore provided the Tiverton school with a portrait of Blundell, their founder. Unfortunately, it was lost in transit.[38] If this date is correct, the donor is likely to have been Sir William, the second Whitmore baronet, living between 1636–1699, a great-grandson, of the merchant adventurer, William Whitmore. At a much later date the school received a print of a portrait from Robert Newton Incledon[39] given under the assumption that it was a likeness of Peter Blundell. The print bears the inscription *'From a portrait given by Thomas Whitmore of Apley Park b. 1782 to Robert Newton Incledon Esq., & by him to the Trustees of the School.'* There is, however, some controversy over the authenticity and date of this portrait. The costume is of the Stuart era, a hundred years later than the Tudor-wear of Peter Blundell himself. It is thought the Whitmores knew other members of the Blundell family and that this portrait might be one of them, or it could even have been one of the Whitmores.[40]

This was how William Whitmore, born in Claverley, Shropshire became a merchant adventurer living in London. But what of his close relations and in-laws? How did William Bond from Somerset come to be in the great metropolis and how did cousin Simon Bourman from Devon become a resident of Spain? What brought the Cornishman, Richard Daniell to the Netherlands and how did Reynold Copcott of London turn out to be a trusted agent in Antwerp of Francis Walsingham? The following chapters outline the lives and events of these men and their families, as well as some of their relationships and friends, describing what they did and how they came to be related to William Whitmore.

---

[38] *Donations of Peter Blundell, Founder and Other Benefactors to the Free ...* By Peter Blundell Google Books.

[39] Robert Newton Incledon was born 1761.

[40] Devon Notes and Queries; Volume 3 J.G. Commin 1905
http://books.google.co.uk/books?id=FLgVAAAAYAAJ&dq=%22William+Whitmore%22+++Haberdasher&q=Whitmore#search_anchor.

William Bond 1524–1576

Crosby Moran Hall (courtesy of Dr Christopher Moran)

Crosby Moran Hall (courtesy of Dr Christopher Moran)

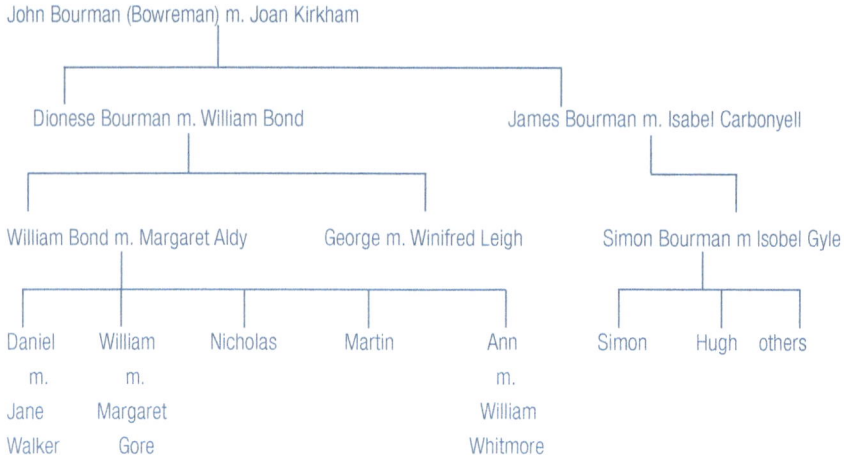

Events during his life time

- 1547 Ivan the Terrible crowned tsar of Russia
- 1553 Search for the Northeast passage
- 1558 England lost Calais to France
- 1564 William Shakespeare baptised
- 1565 Royal Exchange founded by Thomas Gresham
- 1566–1648 Eighty Years' War between Spain and the Netherlands
- 1568 Revolt of the Netherlands
- 1577 Francis Drake's world voyage

William Bond, famed for his seafaring adventures and trading activities, was born in Buckland, Somerset, around the same time as his son-in-law, William Whitmore.[v] He was the eldest son of William Bond and Dionese Bourman from the Somerset branch of the ancient Bond family of Cornwall and Bourman family of Devon. William lived in London and besides his merchandising activities he was a founding member of the Company of Merchant Adventurers to New Lands, formed to find other trading routes and markets. As he rose within the aldermanry of the City he met and married Margaret Aldy, daughter of William Aldy of Guildford. Taking the birth dates of their children into account, they were married around 1549/50.

Although William Bond's life covers the same period as that of William Whitmore, it provides another perspective of that era and shows how the merchant adventurers responded to the political situation in the Lowlands that disrupted their trade and how Queen Elizabeth reacted to the hostility of King Philip II of Spain.

William Bond and Margaret Aldy – Who They Were

William and his brother Sir George Bond are sometimes recorded as the sons of Robert Bond of Trull in Somerset. This is a mistake. The church registers covering several centuries, including the period of the earlier Bonds, have been lost and because of this the genealogical trees of this family hold discrepancies. Fortunately, wills and other records provide conclusive data. The accepted genealogy records that Robert Bond of Beauchamp Hache, the grandfather of William and George Bond, had two sons, Robert and William. While Robert became the ancestor of the Bond branch at Creech and Tyneham in Dorset, William and George of this history were the sons of his younger brother, William.

William's mother, Dionese Bourman, was descended from John Bourman and Joan Birkman/Kirkham of Hemyock, Devon. John Bourman's family came from Brook, Isle of Wight. His widowed great-grandmother, Joan Bowreman, had proved such a genial host to King Henry VII in 1499 he presented her with his drinking horn and a warrant for a fat buck from his forest at Carisbrooke to be provided annually for as long as she lived.[41] The Bourman family of Hemyock is sometimes referred to as Bowerman, or Bowreman, pronounced Boarman, like the boars on the coat of arms. John was the maternal grandfather of William Bond, the elder and paternal grandfather of Simon Bourman of this history.[42]

The very early history of the Bond family rests upon three theories; firstly, and romantically, that the Bond name derives from the Viking Bonders of Norway, a Bonder being the equivalent of a baron today. In Scandinavia, these Bonders had considerable power and owed allegiance solely to the king rather than an overlord. When King Harald Fairhair decided to change to the feudal system the Bonders would have none of it. Proud and independent, they refused to serve under anyone other than the king himself and

---

[41] Brook Village History
https://www.brookvillagehistory.co.uk/early-history/154-the-bowermans
'Parishes: Brook', in *A History of the County of Hampshire: Volume 5*, ed. William Page (London, 1912), pp. 215–217. *British History Online*
http://www.british-history.ac.uk/vch/hants/vol5/pp215–217 [accessed 16 May 2021].

[42] Joan Bowreman of the Isle of Wight bequeathed Brook to her grandson Nicholas, the father of John of Hemyock. The estate included Farringford which would become the home of the poet laureate Alfred Tennyson.

emigrated instead to Iceland, Europe and England. Some of these English Bonders are said to have settled first at Penryth in Cornwall and later at St. Erth in the same county, not far from Penzance.

Surrounded by wildflower meadows and the peaceful reaches of a small rush-fringed river, overgrown with briars of dog rose and blackberries, the tiny village of Erth is one of timeless charm. This was the ancient home of the d'Erth family, living there since the reign of Edward III.[43] The Bonders' descendant Robert Bond married Elizabeth d'Erth, daughter and heiress of Sir Geoffrey d'Erth, at St. Stephen's, near Saltash, Cornwall. These two are the first of the recorded Bond family ancestors.[44]

DNA testing of some members of the Bond family, for what it is worth so far back in time, has proved positive for Viking ancestry, but since the Normans were of Viking descent, the Viking DNA may come from the second more likely hypothesis that the earliest Bond ancestors in this region were Norman incomers, rather than Bonders. The Normans arrived in England at the time of the conquest and one is said to have married a Saxon, from whom Robert Bond descended.

The third suggestion is that the name Bond derives from the Saxon term Bondsman, that is, a peasant bound to a lord. If the first Bond was a Saxon, yet held land after the conquest, he would have been one of the very few Saxons permitted to do so and must have been a man of some importance. Furthermore, recent research on English DNA apparently reveals that the Vikings and Normans rarely married outside their own kin although that result may depend upon the extent of the research.

There is no conclusive proof about the earliest Bond ancestors so whatever the pre and post-conquest history may be, by using documentary evidence the accepted Bond ancestors from the time of Edward III are Elizabeth, heiress of Erth, and Robert Bond. From these early antecedents in Cornwall, branches of the family established themselves in Berkshire, Somerset, Dorset and London, the senior branch remaining in Cornwall. The Bonds of this history are from Somerset and London.

Having determined William's ancestry, what about his wife's? The maternal line is just as revealing as the paternal. Little information is available about her father other than he lived and worked in Guildford, Surrey and his antecedents are regarded as unknown but the memorial plaque for William Bond and Margaret Aldy holds clues. Beside the shield

---

[43] Daniel Lysons and Samuel Lysons, *Magna Britannia: Volume 3, Cornwall* (London, 1814), *British History Online* http://www.british-history.ac.uk/magna-britannia/vol3 [accessed 26 February 2021].

[44] The Bonds of Newbury and London.

from William's coat of arms there is a lozenge-shaped shield above the effigy of Margaret and her daughter. This shape of shield applies to a woman. Margaret, therefore, was the offspring of an armorial family and entitled to her own coat of arms. The lozenge shape on the memorial also implies widowhood. Her husband's will referred to sisters in Kent, which could mean Margaret also hailed from that area.

The devices on Margaret's shield are very similar to those of the Aldy family of Sandwich and Ash in Kent.[45] Wills are a good source of family connections and those of the Aldy/Alde/Aldye/Alday family (spelt variously for each member of the family) reveal valuable information. From the will of Thomas Aldy, a grocer and gentleman of Ash, it can be deduced that he had two brothers, William and John. He left a bequest to nephew, Henry Allday/Aldey, a mayor of Canterbury and son of his brother, William. The three brothers were merchants and William, Margaret's father, was responsible for the produce sent from Kent to London. Henry, mayor of Canterbury 1560, was therefore her brother.[vi]

The Aldy name is of Anglo-Saxon origin. Dating from the early fourteenth century, the Aldy family were land-owning merchants, MPs and mayors of Dover and Sandwich. They imported their wares, particularly wool, from Calais, Sluis and Middelburg in Zeeland into the pretty little Elizabethan Cinque Port[46] of Sandwich and from there to London.[47]

Because of their knowledge of overseas ports and countries, sovereigns would call upon the services of merchants. Calais and the surrounding district belonged to England and in 1523 Henry VIII, eager to enforce his entitlement to the French crown, decided to invade France. He required 500 men to serve in France as soldiers, led by the duke of Suffolk. A man named Copuldyke was sent by the high marshal of Calais, Sir Edward Guildford, to ask Thomas Aldy to find, *'the tallest men that be in their parties.'*[48] This was the beginning of Henry's expansionist aims, which culminated in the fall of England's economy and the misfortune suffered by John Johnson as described in an earlier chapter.

---

[45] Aldy/Alday shield – red shield, with an ermine chevron between three griffins segreant of the second, those in chief respecting each other. See General Armory of England, Scotland and Wales by John Burke.

[46] The Cinque Ports were south-eastern ports formed in Anglo-Saxon times to 'provide ships'. They continued to be involved in ship building and repair, fishing and piloting until the coastline changed.

[47] Collections for a history of Sandwich in Kent: With notices of the other Cinque Ports and members, and Richborough.

[48] *The Calais Garrison: War and Military Service in England*, 1436–1568 by David Grummitt.

Today, Sandwich is no longer a port. Gradually, over four and half centuries, the sea receded and the town now lies a mile or two inland from the mouth of the river Stour.

William Bond – The Merchant's Tale

William Bond and his brother Sir George Bond became members of the Haberdashers' Company in London by patrimony. The brothers grew up in London where they developed their City and merchandising futures, and their descendants settled. William developed trade in French and Lowland ports as well as venturing to other domains as a merchant adventurer, while Sir George Bond, also a merchant, chose a more civic path, rising through the aldermanry to become lord mayor of London covering the period of the Spanish Armada. Sir George was to become the ancestor of the first duke of Marlborough and Viscount Melbourne, Queen Victoria's first prime minister through his marriage to Winifred Leigh. Some of the offspring of merchant adventurer, William Whitmore also became related to the Leigh family; yet more evidence of the inter-relationship of the merchants and aldermanry.

Margaret and William Bond had four living sons, Daniel, William, Nicholas, and Martin and a daughter, Ann Bond, the wife of William Whitmore of the previous chapter. The Bond memorial depicts at least seven children, but two died in childhood. All four sons followed in the footsteps of their father and uncle as merchants and City worthies.

Their father exported broadcloth, to the wool staple at Antwerp, in exchange for a wide variety of imports. Antwerp, a lively, ancient market town, the hub of culture; rich in music, art, printing and tailoring was a central venue for wealthy merchants to acquire the accoutrements of prosperity: tapestries, books and paintings with which to adorn their homes. They also chose Antwerp tailors to fashion their clothes. Trading here, however, was not a straightforward activity in this period. The Lowlands and the staple of Antwerp were riven with rivalry and political interference. The German and Baltic towns of the Hanseatic League (Hansard, Hansa or Easterlings) had a trade monopoly inland and along the coast of Northern Europe from the Baltic to the North Sea. They also obtained trading advantages not afforded to their English competitors. To make matters worse, in England they had the same rights of trade as the English merchants. This enabled the Hansa to compete with an unfair advantage and undersell the English. For 600 years the German merchants lived in England as a separate and independent community just behind what is now Cannon Street Station, London. Their warehouses and trading facilities, called the Steelyard, were situated on the north bank of the Thames by the outflow of the River Walbrook. Such a greedy monopoly created resentment within England and the Low Countries. The English merchant adventurers struggled valiantly to gain economic mastery of the German markets but had to concede defeat and withdrew from Germany and Scandinavia to trade at other Lowland ports and Antwerp. It was not until the reign of Edward VI that Hanseatic domination began to be curbed.

On the death of Henry VIII in 1547 his sole male heir, the ailing Protestant Edward, became King Edward VI at the tender age of ten. The highly intelligent and very well educated Edward, although very young, took an active interest in the affairs of state aided by his advisers, one of whom was the maternal Bourman relation, John Russell, first Earl of Bedford. The Privy Council and the merchant adventurers persuaded Edward to revoke the Hansa's privileges, thus allowing the English merchants to trade on equal terms with other overseas merchants. By acceding to this request, Edward began, but died too soon to complete the process of ensuring the ascendency of England's merchant trade against the Hansa. The completion would become the legacy of his half-sister, Queen Elizabeth I.

The Hansa were now somewhat restrained but it was not the end of the merchant adventurers' difficulties. By 1550 onwards, another nation sought control in the Lowland markets. The powerful Spanish had control of the Spanish Netherlands and with it the wool staple in Antwerp. Spanish affluence, which derived from the plunder of gold from the Inca conquest, would, before long, bring about Spain's downfall, but in the meantime it allowed her to fight wars of domination against Protestant nations. Such unrest damaged English trading activities and hindered William Bond and other merchants. This unfair Hanseatic advantage and other problems in the Lowlands may have spurred William Bond to diversify by trading further afield.

Trade, however, requires the development of stable markets. William Bond and William Whitmore had recognised that although Edward VI had revoked some of the Hansa's trading advantages their stranglehold over trade in Northern Europe severely restricted England's commercial and economic strength. That situation would not be fully resolved until 1598 when Queen Elizabeth closed the London Steelyard, the trading base of the Hanseatic League, but by then both William Bond and William Whitmore were dead. Prior to that, although the exchange of trade between England and the Netherlands ideally suited each other – the Netherlands buying most of the English exports in return for supplying the majority of England's imports – it was not enough. This difficulty, compounded by the Lowlands thirty-year war and Spain's control of the wool trade in the Netherlands, created unstable merchandising conditions. Something had to be done.

It became essential for England to expand her enterprise and find other trading partners elsewhere. But first, Portugal and Spain's domination of the seas with their large, well-fortified galleons had to be overcome because their *'letter marque tem of mare clausum'* unfairly gave them a monopoly of the seas. That is, the sea came under their jurisdiction and was thus inaccessible to other nations. A *letter of marque* for the English would allow the armed ships of the merchants and their sailors to form a naval flotilla for use in warfare and break Spanish and Portuguese control.

The secret of success is to find opportunity in the face of adversity. This William Bond did. There was more to the Bond family than merchandising and governance; they also had a maritime history, and William a questing nature.

The beginnings of the English navy had been assembled by Henry VII decades before. A strong navy was essential to safeguard England's shores from pillage and her people from being captured and sold into slavery by Barbary pirates. The navy had also to protect merchant vessels from interference by other nations' privateers. These privateers, lured by the immense riches borne by merchant ships – riches that sometimes equalled the wealth of a small nation – acted with the tacit agreement of their monarch, thereby enriching themselves, their crew and their nation's treasury. Skulduggery reigned on the high seas and Tudor England was no angel in this respect. Ongoing hostilities, some perpetrated by Henry VIII, had persuaded him to strengthen his father's navy. He also encouraged people to build their own ships to augment the nation's fleet. This fitted with the Bonds' seafaring activities. They built, owned and part-owned several fast, armed merchant ships for their own mercantile use, namely the *Barke Bond*, the *Valentyne*, the *Fortune*, *Jonas*, and the *Primrose* (part-owned by John Hawkins, privateer and naval commander) and others.

The race was on to discover new routes for trade in gold, spices and fine cloth from the East Indies and to locate other outlets for the declining export of English cloth. In this the merchant adventurers were aided by the curiosity of British explorers to discover and map what lay beyond the horizon. Hitherto, goods from the Orient were mainly transported using the ancient silk trading routes followed by the great Venetian explorer Marco Polo three centuries earlier.

Marco Polo had written of Cathay (China), a rich land of palaces, their treasure rooms, filled with gold, silver and precious stones. The gleaming domes of the palaces, brilliant green, blue and red, could be seen from afar.[49] The imports from China and the Spice Islands travelled by camel caravans overland through Uzbekistan, the Black Sea and thence to the ancient Grand

---

[49] The medieval name for China, as used by Marco Polo.

Bazaar at Constantinople (Istanbul), onward to Venice and thence to the rest of Europe. The usual sea route was long and hazardous. Protected by gunboats and armed merchant brigs, a shorter sea route would be quicker and safer, but did a shorter passage exist? The Spanish cartographer Sebastian Cabot thought so. In 1551 the Company of Merchant Adventurers for the Discovery of Regions, Dominions, Islands and Places Unknown was established, founded by Richard Chancellor, Sebastian Cabot and Sir Hugh Willoughby.

In an effort to protect their future business, the founding members, consisting of the leading overseas merchants, sought to prevent non-company merchants from receiving any profits from trading in cloth. Among these founding members were the twenty-six-year-olds William Bond and William Whitmore. This 'closed shop' was not entirely motivated by self-interest. Over-trading would damage the English market, including the home production of cloth, and such a risky investment had to cover costs and provide good returns. Several other members of the Whitmore and Bond families, as well as families related to them, traded either in mainland Europe or took part in the expansion of exploration and commerce further afield.[50] By risking their fortune, these adventurers sometimes made losses, some became bankrupt, but the best of them amassed great fortunes.

To accomplish their ambition of discovery the merchants had somehow to out-sail the opposition. Faster ships would help. The full-rigged, speedy merchantmen and brigs of the Somerset Bond family gave them an advantage, but a new and quicker route to the East would provide an even greater lead over their competitors and less interference from their privateers.

Could they find this speedier trading route to the Far East and the oriental marvels through a sea passage round Scandinavia and Russia, instead of round the coast of Africa they wondered? It was worth a try, and in 1553 about 240 London merchants and ship-owners, including William Bond,[51] financed an expedition to discover this passage. Such was William's

---

[50] The families of Bond, Bourman (sometimes referred to as Bowerman or Bowreman), and other related merchants.

[51] *Trade between England and Russia in the Second Half of the Sixteenth Century* T. S. Willan The English Historical Review, Vol. 63, No. 248 (Jul., 1948), pp. 307–321. This article consists of 15 page(s).
http://links.jstor.org/sici?sici=0013-8266%28194807%2963%3A248%3C307% 3ATBEARI%3E2.0.CO%3B2-M&size=LARGE&origin=JSTOR-enlargePage See also TS Willan, *The Muscovy Merchants of 1555* (Manchester University Press, 1953); TS Willan, *The Early History of the Russia Company, 1553–1603* (Manchester University Press, 1956); and AG Cross, 'Chaplains to the British Factory in St Petersburg, 1723–1813', *European Studies Review 2*, no 2 (1972), pp125–142. Copies of all of these are available at Guildhall Library.

contribution, the government owed him over £7,000 (worth over £3,000,000 today). Unusually, some years later, a woman member joined the company: the widowed Margarett Bond, almost certainly William's wife whom he had instructed in his will to carry on trading, if she wished. Dr John Dee, the man credited with Humphrey Llwyd, antiquarian and map-maker for coining the expression 'British Empire' excelled in navigation and he became an adviser to the Muscovy Company, later named the Russia Company. Ships, now sturdier than their predecessors, made the venture more feasible but it was still a hazardous business; a venture only made possible by the entrepreneurial spirit of the funders willing to risk their capital in the hope of greater rewards, and the sailors prepared to tolerate and risk their lives in the austere conditions and danger such voyages entailed.

Seal of the Arms of the Muscovy Company, 1555[52]

Three ships, the *Bona Esperanza*, the *Bona Confidentia* and the *Edward Bonaventure*, led by Sir Hugh Willoughby and Richard Chancellor, set sail from the Thames in 1553. At Greenwich Palace, the ailing Edward VI watched as the vessels receded into the distance. Seeking the Northeast Passage was a braver mission than they might have guessed. The sailors fought biting winds as their ships tossed on the icy waves whipped up in the inhospitable waters of the north. Such harsh conditions take their victims.

Of the three ships just one was successful. Nothing more was heard of the crews from the *Bona Esperanza* and *Bona Confidentia*. They were thought to have perished, trapped by ice in the frozen wastes of a northern winter; a fate that seemed conclusive when Russian fishermen in 1554 found the two ships and their lifeless crew north of the Arctic Circle on the desolate shores near Murmansk. Despite the finding of a will, dated January 1554, which showed that they were still alive after seven months, death from scurvy, cold or starvation became the accepted theories.

The third ship, the *Edward Bonaventure*, under the command of Richard

---

[52] Wikipedia . https://en.wikipedia.org/wiki/Muscovy_Company.

Chancellor, survived the storms that had driven the others off-course and he found safe haven at the mouth of the Dvina at Archangel; a port still in use by the nineteenth-century 'jute barons' of Dundee. Tsar Ivan IV, 'Ivan the Terrible,' or more correctly 'formidable', had invited Chancellor to Moscow and Chancellor now made the long and arduous 1,000-kilometre journey by horse-drawn sleigh to the capital, not knowing what dangers he might encounter on the way. It was a wonderful feat of endurance but a journey worth the difficulty. Chancellor received a warm welcome and beheld a wooden palace of lavish comfort and magnificence, though much of the population of Moscow endured primitive housing after two disastrous fires in 1547 had destroyed a large proportion of the town, which led to widespread poverty.

A hundred years later, the description of the court is rather different. Pepys' diary, 12 September 1664, describes Russia and its court as poor. *'Mr. Pargiter says, Russia is a sad place; and, though Moscow is a very great city, yet it is from the distance between house and house, and few people compared with this, and poor, sorry houses, the Emperor himself living in a wooden house, his exercise only flying a hawk at pigeons and carrying pigeons ten or twelve miles off and then laying wagers which pigeon shall come soonest home to her house.'*

A surprising description considering Chancellor's remarks, but a hundred years later, housing expectations were probably higher and a lot can happen over a hundred years. During that time, Moscow had suffered battles, famine, plague and fires but we know, nevertheless, from other historical descriptions, that there were buildings of architectural significance.

Although Chancellor and his crew had failed to find a passage through to Cathay, they had found Russia, and were the first Englishmen to set foot in that country. Chancellor developed a good rapport with the recently crowned twenty-two-year-old tsar and struck an agreement allowing English merchants to trade with Russia and her trading partners. Furthermore, they could keep control of any English settlement that may develop there in the future. The voyage is commemorated by a memorial plaque originally sited at Rotherhithe Park, but is now incorporated in the overhead structure of Rotherhithe tunnel, London.

Having secured a lucrative trade deal with Russia, the voyage was considered a worthy investment, despite the loss of two vessels, and on 26 February, 1555 the Muscovy Company was formally incorporated by royal charter.[53]

Later that year two vessels, the *Edward Bonaventure*, with Richard Chancellor aboard, and the *Philip and Mary* made a second voyage to Russia. The *Philip and Mary* was to stop at Vardo to collect a cargo of fish

---

[53] *Guildhall MSS* http://www.history.ac.uk/gh/russia.htm

oil while Chancellor on the *Edward* was to obtain permission from Tsar Ivan to set up warehouses in Moscow or other towns.

The Russians had restored *Bona Confidentia* and *Bona Esperanza* and these vessels joined the flotilla for the return voyage back to England. It was a disaster. Beset by violent storms, of the four vessels of the fleet only one battered ship returned home. She was the *Philip and Mary*. Having overwintered in Trondheim she limped homeward in 1557. One of the restored ships was wrecked on rocks off Norway, the other was never seen again. Richard Chancellor and the *Edward Bonaventure* had survived the perils that beset the others until 10 November, 1556. Then, while rounding the treacherous coast of Scotland during another storm, the ship foundered on rocks off Rosehearty. The tsar's ambassador, aboard with a treasure trove for Queen Mary, was cast with the rest of the crew into the raging sea. Miraculously, the ambassador survived with some staff due to a heroic attempt by Richard Chancellor to reach shore in a small boat, but Chancellor lost his own life in the swamped vessel.

The Scots found the ambassador and a few other survivors and confined them all for several months. Of the treasure, nothing more was seen or heard. Suspecting mischief, the Herald of Arms made repeated threats to the locals. Flotsam from wreckage often finds its way to the shore but this was a mysterious tale of booty apparently 'lost' to the depths of the ocean for eternity; an incident reminiscent of the novel *Whisky Galore*, a twentieth century fictional tale of a community's connivance to purloin a missing cargo of whisky. In the year 2000, a survey of the rocky seabed, though difficult, yielded no evidence of the ship or anything else.

Three vessels had now perished in the waters of the north but it was not the last that was heard of the *Bona Esperanza* and her first voyage to Russia. Over 400 years after the 1555 event, a letter came to light, addressed to the doge of Venice from Giovanni Michiel, Venetian ambassador to Britain. This indicated that the bodies of the crew from the first voyage to Russia had been discovered in attitudes suggesting they were in the act of performing tasks, unaware of the sudden demise that was about to befall them. This points to the entire crew having died of carbon monoxide poisoning, a not uncommon occurrence when people light fires, close off all ventilation and huddle together for warmth. This is a credible hypothesis because the ship carried plenty of woollen clothing and coal, and Willoughby's diary recorded that searches for habitation had proved fruitless but there was an abundance of wildlife for food. They also had access to sea coal along the shore, a source of further heat, but also of carbon monoxide when burnt.[54]

---

[54] *The Fate of Sir Hugh Willoughby and His Companions: A New Conjecture* Eleanora C. Gordon *The Geographical Journal*, Vol. 152, No. 2 (Jul., 1986), pp. 243–247. See JSTOR doi:10.2307/634766. This article consists of 5 page(s).

Though the Muscovy Company had sustained heavy losses – several ships, the very valuable Russian cargo of furs, jewels and other gifts, plus the lives of the intrepid and valued Chancellor and Willoughby, as well as other merchants and the crew, trade between Russia and England continued to the benefit of both.

The young King Edward VI had died aged just sixteen shortly after the ships set sail for the Northeast Passage but he had left a trading legacy, which set in train the birth of an empire. If only Edward's health had matched his intellect, England might have avoided some of the internal religious strife that ensued during the reigns of his two half-sisters who succeeded him. First the bloody but mercifully short reign of the Catholic Mary I, known as bloody Mary that brought death to Protestants openly opposed to the Catholic faith. Mary's Protestant half-sister, Elizabeth I, succeeded in 1558 and that again brought England into conflict, this time with Catholic countries keen to impose their own doctrine. How much better might Europe have prospered had the countries of Europe not become embattled because of their religious difference and grievance?

The rest of William Bond's merchandising took place in the reign of Elizabeth I. Trade with Russia continued to be successful. It served William Bond well, until he fell out with the Russia Company, the renamed Muscovy Company, by trading on his own account with Narva.[55] It was a bold move considering that the Russia Company's charter permitted it to seize the ships and merchandise of anyone caught illicitly trading within the company's designated territories. The Russia Company made a complaint to the Privy Council about William's right to trade independently. William, his brother Sir George Bond, and John Foxall a fellow merchant, argued that since the Russia Company did not discover Narva, it did not fall within the Company's jurisdiction and their trading was not prejudicial to the Company.[56, 57] This argument was not accepted and on 7 November 1564 Queen Elizabeth ordered that William be thrown into the Fleet prison for a week for contemptuously trading with Narva contrary to the

---

[55] The North Atlantic of the Seventeenth Century.

[56] Foxall was a London mercer. He was a founder of the Eastland Company in 1579, to trade with Scandanavia. William Bond's widow, Margaret was the only woman member.

[57] MS British Library Cotton Nero B. viii. Not dated. Datable to 1564; the dispute was heard by the Privy Council on 14 Dec. 1564 [Acts of the Privy Council, n.s. VII, 1558–70, pp. 178–9]. Willan, 'The Russia Company and Narva 1558–81', p. 407, follows Cal. S. P. Dom. in dating it 25 November 1564. Copy P.R.O., SP 12/35, art. 21 (dated 25 November 1564) *Calendar of State Papers, Domestic Series,of the Reigns of Edward Vi., Mary, Elizabeth.*

commandment given by the board.⁵⁸,⁵⁹ The experience made an impression on William and is reflected in the drafting of his will.

On his release, William continued with his European merchandising, using his own vessels as well as hiring them out for use by other merchants. He traded in Spain, France, Belgium and the Netherlands. The trade documents of the London port for 1567–68 give details of his imports. Prunes from Rouen, Nantes and Bordeaux; coarse hat wool, Spanish wool and sackcloth from Antwerp; raisins and almonds from Marbella; Gascony wine from Bordeaux; flax from Amsterdam; bastards and cuit from Ayamonte (biscuit); canvas from Rouen; aniseed from Port St. Mary; butts sacks from Cadiz; and Coniac (Cognac) wine from a source not mentioned.⁶⁰

As can be seen, this produce came mostly from ports outside the Netherlands reflecting the disruption there. Yet again, the Netherland trade was in turmoil, or at least the English merchants were because of the ever-recurring Spanish and English squabbles. In December 1567, the duke of Alva had seized and confined the English merchants in the Netherlands, causing a breakdown of trade in her ports. Then, in early 1568 the Netherlands revolted. The Revolt of the Netherlands began the Eighty Years War.⁶¹ Many inhabitants of the Netherlands were executed and tens of thousands fled. Following several incidents between Spain and England that year, the exasperated Queen Elizabeth closed all trade between Spain and England. Nevertheless, England benefited. Refugees escaping to peaceful London brought their well-honed skills and knowledge to the capital and that enabled lagging London to flourish. Bookshops opened filled with literature, hitherto in short supply, and craftsmanship expanded. Antwerp's loss was London's gain and she never looked back.

Regardless of the problems in previous years, mercantile activities in Europe and Spain had proved fruitful for William. The Russia Company had delivered handsome dividends and William's civic career was on the ascent. In 1566 he was elected auditor for the commissioners of excise, and alderman and sheriff of London in 1567-1568.⁶² As sheriff he attended the lord mayors, Sir Roger Martin and Sir Thomas Rowe, during their official

---

⁵⁸ *The life and times of Sir Thomas Gresham by Burgon John William*

⁶⁰ Elizabethan Port and Trade Documents with information about the Bond family trading. *http://www.british-history.ac.uk/report.asp?compid=35953*

⁶¹ Sometimes referred to as the Dutch War of Independence, began as a revolt of the Seventeen Provinces against Philip II of Spain, the sovereign of the Habsburg Netherlands.

⁶² *The Aldermen of the City of London, vol. II* by the Rev. Alfred B. Beaven, Eden Fisher & Co., Ltd., London, 1913.

engagements, took part in sessions at the Central Criminal Court at the Old Bailey and presented petitions from the City to Parliament at the bar of the House of Commons. During his term of office, the rise of Puritanism gave cause for concern and the Privy Council requested that Bishop Grindal confer with William Bond for the best way of ensuring religious uniformity.

As an alderman he would have had assets of at least £10,000, (over £1.5 million today), £10,000 being the minimum demanded of an alderman if elected as lord mayor of London. Each mayor had to self-finance civic hospitality and pageantry.

As a rising governor of the City, now was the time for William Bond to consolidate his considerable assets and acquire the trappings of achievement. William purchased the magnificent Crosby Place in Bishopsgate, sometimes referred to erroneously as Crosby Palace. The mansion had been created by the merchant John Crosby in the mid-1460s from the fifteenth-century buildings of Bishopsgate and included the Great Hall. William increased its imposing structure with the addition of a turret, creating an illustrious addition to his standing as sheriff and leading adventurer.

This residence had a distinguished past. It had been the home of Richard III when Duke of Gloucester in 1483, and Shakespeare, who knew the building well, as a resident of St. Helen's parish,[63] placed Crosby Hall as the setting for Richard's plotting in his play, Richard III. The building evidently stimulated the imagination. Earlier, but in contrast to Shakespeare's sinister tale, Sir Thomas More had been stirred to write updated versions to his *Utopia* while living there in 1516.

As century followed century, knowledge of Crosby Place's historic past faded from public memory and it fell prey to the vagaries of fashion and a disregard for its architectural significance, history and grandeur. Gradually, much of Crosby Place, apart from the Great Hall, was demolished. The expense of maintenance may also have played a part. Even the Great Hall, like a withered bloom, slowly disintegrated until threatened by demolition in the early twentieth century. Such a threat galvanised interest in one of the City's most ancient buildings, and stone by stone, like a phoenix, it arose from decrepitude. It was re-erected in Danvers Street, west of Chelsea Church, to be used as a dining hall and residence by the British Federation of University Women. More recently, at the end of the twentieth century, a philanthropist keenly interested in the history of London and the buildings of its past but saddened by all that

---

[63] Assessment rolls for subsidies in 1598. William Shakespeare as taxpayer and tax defaulter https://shakespearedocumented.folger.edu/node/941

has been lost in order to accommodate commerce, industry and population, decided to save at least one threatened building as a reminder of London's rich history. He is Dr Christopher Moran and he undertook the amazing 30-year task of restoring the magnificent fifteenth-century Crosby Hall to its former glory. One only has to look on the website below to realise how huge a project it has been.[64] To maintain its Tudor and Stuart authenticity, all the ornately carved wood and stone-work, plastered ceilings and cornices inlaid with blue and gold, polished floors and vast windows incorporating decorative motifs had to be researched, and skilled and knowledgeable craftsmen and women found, to recreate the hall's structure using authentic methods and materials and furnishing. The exterior is as impressive as the interior. The recreated parterre gardens and fountains are just as they would have looked in those bygone days. Plants that would have been familiar to our Tudor ancestors complete the scene.[65]

In William's time Crosby Hall was a suitably grand residence for entertaining – or 'detaining' – dignitaries on behalf of the monarch. It was here that William 'entertained' the duke of Alva's agent, d'Assonleville who was on a mission to retrieve missing bullion.[66]

During the Revolt of the Netherlands, in 1568, led by William of Orange, five Spanish galleons carrying £85,000 of gold bullion to pay the duke of Alva's army in the Netherlands, had sheltered from storms in an English port. With the likelihood of pirates seeking treasure ships along the coast of England, Queen Elizabeth ordered the bullion's removal from the vessels for 'safekeeping'. Such was the antipathy between England and Spain, it was a move that predictably invited Spanish suspicion of duplicity on the part of the Queen. It was certainly an astute political move by Elizabeth. Unpaid Spanish soldiers would be unlikely to attack England. The Spanish ambassador, Don Guerau de Spes, accused the queen of seizing the gold but this bullion did not belong to Spain, it was on loan to the Spanish by the Genoese, so technically Elizabeth was merely taking on that loan. When

---

[64] Crosby Hall https://www.christophermoran.org/crosby-hall/photos-of-crosby-hall/
[65] *Crosby Hall – The Most Important Surviving Domestic Medieval Building In London* by Dr. Simon Thurley, Director of English Heritage. This gives an account of the move and rebuilding of Crosby Hall, its architecture and features, which include some used at Chastleton House, Oxfordshire, a residence that belonged to the Whitmore Jones family.
[66] Philip Norman and W D Caroe, 'The history of Crosby Place', in *Survey of London Monograph 9, Crosby Place* (London, 1908), pp. 15-32. *British History Online* http://www.british-history.ac.uk/survey-london/bk9/pp15-32 [accessed 11 November 2021].

the duke of Alva's agent d'Assonleville came to London in 1569 to demand the return of the bullion, William Bond played host and custodian. Was it mockery on the part of Elizabeth I to house d'Assonleville amongst English merchants, whose trade the Spanish had disrupted? Elizabeth had seized the initiative. The intervention of d'Assonleville's gained little. D'Assonleville complained that the queen prevented him from meeting with the Spanish ambassador, based only a short distance from Crosby Place, and refused to grant him an audience. Instead, she held Spain to ransom over its hostilities and the difficulties it caused to English trade in the Low Countries. D'Assonleville returned to Spain empty-handed but with the queen's promise of restitution on condition that the Spanish king guaranteed security to all Elizabeth's subjects in the Low Countries.[67] Though angered by the queen, d'Assonleville had no quarrel with his host. He conceded that the English merchants had treated him well and he had been graciously entertained by William Bond.[68]

Two years later in 1571, terrified by the rise in Protestantism within his realm, the Spanish king activated the Spanish Inquisition to impede such heresy. Yet again, the English merchants trading there suffered disruption, including William Whitmore. The king hoped it would also frustrate the ascendency of the Protestant faith in England. Many English merchants suffered the confiscation of their goods and in 1574 William Bond learnt that his petition for the retrieval of 1,500 ducats owed to him in Seville would not be returned. William sent his factor Lucas de Campos a letter authorised by patent of the Queen of England, ordering the restitution of the monies. Instead, this letter added fuel to the pyre of Anglo–Spanish relations. The document included among the queen's titles that of 'Defender of the Faith', that is Protestant faith, a title that would be sure to inflame the ire of a pious, Catholic king. William's debtor in Seville made full use of the insult. Hoping to escape from paying his dues, he informed the Inquisition of Elizabeth's affront to Catholic sensibilities. The Inquisition reprehended William's factor Lucos de Campos and then passed on the offensive letter to the Spanish king. Outraged and in a fury King Philip sent de Campos

---

[67] 'Rome: 1569, January-June', in *Calendar of State Papers Relating To English Affairs in the Vatican Archives, Volume 1, 1558-1571*, ed. J M Rigg (London, 1916), pp. 291-310. *British History Online* http://www.british-history.ac.uk/cal-state-papers/vatican/vol1/pp291-310 [accessed 19 November 2021].

[68] *The queen's merchants and the revolt of the Netherlands: the end of the Antwerp mart ...* By George Daniel Ramsay

packing empty-handed. William Bond must have wondered if he would ever receive reimbursement.[69,70]

Protracted diplomatic exchanges between the Spanish and English ambassadors followed over the course of two years, and then on 30 December 1576 King Philip ordered the Seville Inquisition to restore the monies held. In future no detentions were to be made on this account – too late for William Bond. The life of this dashing and intrepid adventurer ended on 30 May 1576 at fifty-one years of age – not particularly old compared to many of his fellow merchants, though two of his sons were even younger when they died. Considering that in 1551 thousands of the prosperous died of the horrific 'sweating sickness' that killed within hours, followed by the 1557 influenza epidemic, a cause of the demise of 5% of the nation, plus years of intermittent plague and malaria, it is perhaps amazing that many of the Whitmore and other associated families survived these ravages.

The funeral service for William Bond took a form reminiscent of the old religion; in other words leaning towards the old Catholic Mass for the repose of the soul but dressed up to meet with Protestant ritual. These Somerset and London Bonds evidently held dear to their erstwhile Catholic faith, an irony considering King Philip's actions, but pragmatically they had bowed to the demands of a Protestant monarch. William, as requested, had upheld the national Protestant faith against revised versions. In the years to come this family of Bonds remained true to their monarch and the faith imposed. Not so the Dorset branch of the family. By the reign of Charles I they had become fervent Puritans and supporters of Oliver Cromwell.

William is buried at St. Helen's Church, Bishopsgate, London. The left-hand side of a small monument shows him surrounded by his seven children. Only four sons and a daughter Ann are mentioned in his will and other historical documents, the others having predeceased him. His arms and those of his wife are displayed above the figures. On the right his wife is depicted in a vast sleeved dress with their daughter and above them her coat of arms, *gules* à chevron *argent* between three birds *argent* (griffins) with

---

[69] 'Elizabeth: Miscellaneous, 1574', in *Calendar of State Papers Foreign: Elizabeth, Volume 10, 1572-1574*, ed. Allan James Crosby (London, 1876), pp. 586-591. *British History Online*
http://www.british-history.ac.uk/cal-state-papers/foreign/vol10/pp586-591 [accessed 19 November 2021].

[70] 'Simancas: December 1576', in *Calendar of State Papers, Spain (Simancas), Volume 2, 1568-1579*, ed. Martin A S Hume (London, 1894), pp. 534-538. *British History Online*
http://www.british-history.ac.uk/cal-state-papers/simancas/vol2/pp534-538 [accessed 19 November 2021].

three lozenges *gules* on the chevrons. The full Bond coat of arms and crest sits above the monument of figures.[71] The detail of the crest is poor but it appears to be an elongated image described as a lion as was used in the ancient arms of the Cornish Bonds from whom William descended.[72][73]

Below the figures the following inscription is written:

'Here lyeth the body of William Bond, Alderman and sometime sheriff of London, a merchant adventurer, and most famous in his age for his great adventures both by sea and by land. Obit 30 die Maii, 1576.' A translation of his Latin epitaph reads as follows – 'Behold under this tomb, William Bond, the flower of the merchants which Britain has produced lies buried. He having suffered much amongst waves and rocks, enriched the shores of his country by means of foreign merchandise. Alas that death cannot be bribed with gold! The Flower of Merchants, William Bond, lies buried.'

A British ship captained by a William Bond in 1545 entered the Gulf of Mississippi to be met by the ferocious Washa tribe. To the annoyance of the French, who said they owned the land, this William Bond and his crew successfully fought off the tribe as they negotiated their way up-stream. Could this have been the youthful, adventuring William of the epitaph above? If not, it is likely to have been one of his many seafaring relations.[74]

Buried at the same church are his great friends, Sir Thomas Gresham, Sir John and Lady Spencer and Sir William Pickering.

William left instructions for his wife, Margaret Aldy to carry on the merchandising business and continue to live at Crosby Place unless she remarried. Margaret did not remarry and, with her son William, his wife, Margaret Gore, and brother-in-law Sir George Bond, she carried out her husband's wishes. Very unusually for a woman, she became a charter member of the Eastland Company trading with Sweden and Denmark. This smaller company, although similar to the merchant adventurer companies, had neither their volume of trade nor political influence. She seems also, after William's death, to have been a member of the newly named Russia Company.

---

[71] 'St. Helen's Bishopsgate: Monuments within the church', *Survey of London: volume 9: The parish of St Helen, Bishopsgate, part I* (1924), pp. 52–79. URL: http://www.british-history.ac.uk/report.aspx?compid=98362

[72] *The General Armory of England, Scotland, Ireland, and Wales* By Bernard Burke.

[73] See flickr for larger and clearer photo http://www.flickr.com/photos/stiffleaf/5793729706/.

[74] Chitimacha History http://www.dickshovel.com/chi.html

A generous benefactor of several charities, William included St. Thomas and St. Bartholomew Hospitals in his will. He also provided for all his family, their servants, godchildren, several friends and fellow merchants. As evidence of the close-knit family connections of these adventurers, William's will includes Blaise/Blaze Saunders. Blaise was the brother of Sabine Johnson, wife of John Johnson, the Calais merchant adventurer of this book. Also not forgotten were the masters of his ships, which he names as the *Barke Bond*, the *Valentyne*, the *Primrose*, the *Jonas* and *Fortune*. Poor apprentices and poor students at Oxford University are also beneficiaries. His interest in Oxford University may have been because his son Martin Bond attended St. Alban's College, Oxford.[75] He cancelled debts owed to him and provided a year's free tenancy for the tenants of his properties. William's week in prison had provided him with insight into the plight of those who had fallen on hard times, more often victims of life's cruel circumstances than fecklessness. To these debtors, languishing in penal institutions, he left money to be paid each year until the debt be settled.[76]

Tales of the privateering ventures of William's cousin John Bond indicate that he acquired the *Barke Bond* with which he roamed the seas, capturing treasure ships from the Spanish at the tacit behest of Queen Elizabeth.[77]

William's sons held Crosby Place for several years, using it to accommodate and entertain visiting dignitaries such as the ambassadors of Denmark and France[78] as well as Henry Ramelius, chancellor of Denmark and ambassador to London in 1586.[79] They sold it in 1594 to Sir John Spencer.

During William Bond's lifetime he had provided Queen Elizabeth's impecunious treasury with two six-month loans of £1,000 in November and December 1569. His loan to the government for funding the exploration of the Northeast Passage to China had been a great deal more. William's great friend, Thomas Gresham, the highly accomplished financier of the Antwerp Bourse, also helped to facilitate the merchants' loans to the crown and may have done so for both William Bond and William Whitmore.

---

[75] Oxford Alumni; Oxford Dictionary of National Biography.

[76] An Architectural And Historical Account Of Crosby Place http://www.archive.org/stream/architecturalhis00blaciala/architecturalhis00blaciala_djvu.txt with transcript of will.

[77] *Elizabethan Privateering: English Privateering During the Spanish War, 1585–1603* By Kenneth R. Andrews

[78] Philip Norman and W D Caroe, 'The history of Crosby Place', in *Survey of London Monograph 9, Crosby Place* (London, 1908), pp. 15–32. *British History Online* http://www.british-history.ac.uk/survey-london/bk9/pp15-32 [accessed 26 February 2021].

[79] Crosby Place – Project Gutenburg & John Strype's Survey of London.

Harassment at the hands of Spain was not all that William and other English merchants had endured. The Elizabethan records mention William Bond and his friend John Foxall among the victims of the French pirates of the seas between 1562 and 1579.[80] Between these dates, sometime around 1572, the Bonds' part-owned ship the *Pelican* had been seized by the French pirate Captain Landreau at Bellisle off the Cherbourg peninsular. Nicholas Fishborne and all the ship's company had been killed and the cargo, valued at £4,000, stolen. The government of Brittany knew both the pirate and the receiver of goods and William and his associates spent a great deal of money pursuing the government for reimbursement. On 15 July 1575 William Bond and others wrote to Walsingham requesting that Queen Elizabeth send letters to the French king seeking compensation for the ship's capture. In December his cousin Thomas Bond and other aldermen petitioned the queen again.[81] Compensation was not forthcoming and they resigned themselves to the loss, deciding instead to *'Leave all in the hands of God rather than prosecute any more suits in France.'* But by 1577 the ship may have been retrieved because John Hawkins put forward a proposal in June of that year to sail in her to Constantinople. But was it William Bond's stolen ship? History records several ships named the *Pelican*. There is no record of the retrieval of William Bond's ship from the French and it is not mentioned among the ships owned by William at his death.

The *Pelican*, a galleon, is the name of the flagship in which Sir Francis Drake circumnavigated the globe. Although Drake, Hawkins and Bond were acquainted, Drake's ship was not the Bond-owned vessel. It was most likely the one built at Plymouth in 1576. Drake commenced his circumnavigation of the world carrying out a considerable amount of plundering on the way as well as capturing Spanish galleons off the coast of South America. He re-named the *Pelican* the *Golden Hinde* as a compliment to Sir Christopher Hatton, his patron, the golden Hinde being Sir Christopher's family crest on his coat of arms.[82]

---

[80] 'Queen Elizabeth – Volume 105: July 1575', in *Calendar of State Papers Domestic: Edward VI, Mary and Elizabeth, 1547–80*, ed. Robert Lemon (London, 1856), pp. 500–502. *British History Online*
http://www.british-history.ac.uk/cal-state-papers/domestic/edw-eliz/1547–80/
pp 500–502 [accessed 26 February 2021].

[81] 'Elizabeth: December 1575, 21–31', in *Calendar of State Papers Foreign: Elizabeth, Volume 11, 1575–1577*, ed. Allan James Crosby (London, 1880), pp. 206–224. *British History Online*
http://www.british-history.ac.uk/cal-state-papers/foreign/vol11/pp206–224
[accessed 26 February 2021].

[82] Ships of Discovery and Exploration by Lincoln P Paine.

A somewhat battered table called 'the cupboard' is an interesting relic belonging to the Middle Temple Hall. It stands in the small gallery at one end of the hall. This is the table to which new barristers of the Middle Temple step-up to sign the roll when 'called to the bar.' The table is said to be the hatch cover from the *Pelican*. A chair made from her timbers resides in the Bodleian Library at Oxford University.

As for William Bond's sons, little information has been found regarding Sir Daniel/Danyell Bond(e). This eldest son, died young and before his mother. His epitaph indicates a happy marriage to Jane Walker, also much honoured by her second husband, Sir John Boys of Canterbury, MP and recorder of Canterbury. This marriage provides a window on how families continued to interact over generations. It is likely that Jane came to know Sir John through the Aldy family, Margaret Aldy being her erstwhile mother-in-law. Sir John Boys was related to Margaret Aldy through his grandmother, Elizabeth Aldy. William Bond's sons, William, Nicholas and Martin are described in the following chapters.

It is thought-provoking to note the different attitudes of members of the family towards establishing themselves and their family within their former rural roots. Whereas William Whitmore, like several other rich merchants, bought himself a large estate in Shropshire within the region of his father's manors around Claverley, he nevertheless remained in London. It was his eldest son who re-established the family in Shropshire. William Bond, on the other hand, made no attempt to buy a rural estate, instead he upgraded his London home. Likewise Sir William Craven, husband of William Whitmore's daughter, Elizabeth. They remained in the City. William Craven left money to establish a school in his name in Yorkshire, the county of his forefathers, merely renting a grand London residence. Nonetheless, in his will he instructed his widow to invest in property, which she did extensively, as did their eldest son, William, Lord Craven.

It is touching to note the concern that William Whitmore, his wife Ann and her mother, Margaret Bond (nee Aldy), had for the future of their children after their deaths. William Whitmore exhorts his children, all under twenty-one, *'to be loving to each other and dutiful and obedient towards their mother'*, for whom his affection is evident throughout the will. Margaret Bond's will desires that her good children, three of them then over twenty-one, *'will lovingly agree together as, thanks be to God, they have hitherto done so and that they will be friendly and helpful to each other in all good faith and thou God will bless them.'* She also expresses the wish that they be good to her servants. Margaret was as considerate as her husband towards other members of the family. She left several bequests to nephews and nieces, her sisters and servants. She also mentions Lady Boys, that is Jane, widow of her son, Daniel. Jane is now named as Margaret's cousin, further proof of Margaret's descent from the Aldy family of Sandwich and Ash in Kent. Margaret was buried 23 May 1588 at St. Helen's, Bishopsgate.

As ventures overseas expanded during the succeeding years, William Bond's brigs and barques traded and sometimes plundered round the globe in Spain, Northern Europe, the Americas and Caribbean. Sir Francis Drake, Sir John Hawkins and Simon Bourman of this history, all Devon men, took part.

William and Margaret's old home, the restored Crosby Hall now stands in Chelsea, overlooking the timeless river Thames that has seen London grow from a Roman port to become one of the largest cities of the world. The hall, with its Tudor paintings, tapestries and furniture is a reminder of a time in England's history when the nation took a bold leap forward onto the world stage.

When visiting Crosby Moran Hall, we of the twenty-first century can experience the Tudor era of our ancestors and perhaps feel the shades of the redoubtable, doublet-hosed merchants who lived there. History is important. It informs us of the trials, goals, skills and vision of our ancestors who dared dream of impossible ventures by ignoring danger to achieve great things. What is our vision for the future? On that rests the prospect of our nation and those yet unborn.

If William Bond had experienced problems with Spain, he was not the only member of his family to do so. His son William Bond Jr., his brother Sir George Bond, and Simon Bourman (Bowman/Bowerman) his cousin all experienced hindrance and annoyance. All of these are of course related to the family of the adventurer William Whitmore through his wife Ann Bond.

William Bond (the younger)
ca. 1555–1608/09

Events during his lifetime

- 1576 Search for the Northwest Passage to Cathay
- 1600 Founding of East India Company
- 1603 Queen Elizabeth died
- 1603 James I inherited the English crown
- 1606 Founding of first English colony at Jamestown, North America

William Bond, the younger was born at Crosby Place, the second of four sons. Like his father and three brothers he became a member of the Haberdasher Company and a merchant adventurer. His father had excelled in the world of merchandise and as a governor of the City and, in what would be the closing years of his life, he was making plans for further ventures with young William. Twenty years previously, merchants and explorers had failed to find a Northeast Passage to Cathay but found Russia instead and, after some disastrous mishaps, the new Muscovy Company formed from that expedition had served them well. The terrain so far north was stormy, hard to navigate and for the most part ice-bound; not surprising when one considers that beside its latitude, the northern hemisphere of the sixteenth century was experiencing an extended period of particularly cold winters.

Nevertheless, despite the known difficulties, the urge to find a quicker route to the Orient had never really gone away. Perhaps instead, they could find the elusive Northwest Passage that others had attempted yet failed to find previously. It would be the ultimate prize in a quest to beat the competition. It would also be an opportunity to map another little known area of the globe.

William was eighteen years old when plans were afoot to attempt this bold mission once more. Privateer Martin Frobisher and the leading London merchants gathered at Crosby Place. William joined them and his father to discuss the project and the raising of funds for an expedition led by Frobisher. With the interest and approval of Queen Elizabeth I, by 1576 enough money had been gathered from a number of wealthy merchants, including William Bond the elder, to finance a small fleet of three ships.[83] The three vessels, the *Gabriel*, *Michael* and another pinnace set sail watched by a large crowd gathered along the Thames. The queen watched from Greenwich Palace as the cannons saluted the departing vessels. With sails rigged, they slowly drifted out of sight.

Sailing north by west, it was not long before these ships had to plough their way through the seas of a violent storm. They, nevertheless, reached the island of Friesland intact – or so they thought. These were the early days of navigation and mapping. Navigating by the stars, if they could see them, and using the roughly drawn maps made by earlier explorers, sailors had very little idea of where they really were in these largely unknown waters of the North West. Friesland did not exist. They had found Greenland. They sailed onward but again the north brewed up a tempest, and this time they had also to steer a course through ice. The little pinnace, fast and manoeuvrable in coastal waters, was no match for such an inhospitable clime. Swamped by waves, she sank. Losing sight of the *Gabriel*, the *Michael*, a three or four masted barque, but not a lot larger than the pinnace, reached Labrador but encountered huge banks of ice through which it would be folly to sail and the captain decided to turn back to England while still in one piece. The *Gabriel*, captained by Frobisher, sailed on until in sight of Labrador, but no, it was Baffin Island, which Frobisher named Queen Elizabeth Foreland, in honour of the queen. Frobisher and crew voyaged onward until they met some Inuit who promised to act as guides through the icy strait. Frobisher, sensing danger, warned the crew not to get too close. Disobeying their captain, they were soon to find out why. Five of the crew were taken captive. A search proved fruitless and Frobisher took the leading Inuit as hostage in the hope of forcing the retrieval of the lost sailors. Whether by their own freewill or not, they were never seen again. The unfortunate captive Inuit returned with the ship to London; a squat, short-legged and swarthy stranger, similar to the Tartars, he became a cause of much interest.

Frobisher had not found the Northwest Passage but he had a better understanding of the coastline and he and the crew had found some black rock, which the sailors collected. They returned to England with this treasure, said to be worth £5 per tonne. Some thought the 'rock' was sea coal, a commodity much needed and one that, in harsh winters, the government doled out to the poor. Michael Lok fancied it might be a

---

[83] 'East Indies: July 1576', in *Calendar of State Papers Colonial, East Indies, China and Japan, Volume 2, 1513–1616*, ed. W Noel Sainsbury (London, 1864), pp. 11–12. *British History Online* http://www.british-history.ac.uk/cal-state-papers/colonial/east-indies-china-japan/vol2/pp11–12 [Accessed 27 February 2021].

gold-bearing ore and despite two English assayers declaring it worthless, he took it to an Italian who showed him some gold dust, which he claimed to have discovered within the ore. Such a find galvanised action. Michael Lok informed the queen. Another voyage was funded and off they set, this time with a much larger flotilla. The learned John Dee gave Frobisher advice on useful navigation instruments as well as instruction on their use. Finding the Northwest Passage was now off the agenda. Gold became the objective.

William's father never got to know the outcome of his investment as he had died just before the vessels set sail on their first voyage in 1576. As for his son, whether it was the questing spirit of adventure inherited from his father, or the assumption of a spectacular find, the younger but less experienced William invested £100 (the equivalent of over £20,000 in 2017) in this second venture, which had been granted incorporation as the Company of Cathay.

The fleet, set fair on a following wind, reached 'Friesland' but fog prevented a landing and Frobisher sailed onwards into severe storms until they reached Hall's Island, where they collected the black ore before returning home with 200 tonnes. Assaying this ore took considerable time, money and debate. Nothing was happening and people were becoming restless. Why wait? It was important to establish a presence in the area and repel competitors from the source of such riches. Fuelled by the enthusiasm of Michael Lok, who had persuaded the queen to his cause, a much larger fleet set forth. Braving icebergs and storms they made their way to Frobisher Bay but failed in an attempt to create a colony there because of squabbling and dissent. They did, however, find and collect a quantity of the precious ore. It was a venture doomed to disappoint; a dream that vanished on waking when all that glistered was found not to be gold but hornblende with an appearance of specks of gold, much like iron pyrites, otherwise known as 'fools' gold.' A great deal of money had been lost, the most by Michael Lok, a once-rich man now consigned to the debtors' prison. Young William Bond had wisely decided not to invest in this risky venture before knowing more. The second voyage, after all, had not shown any return. He survived the setback and expense of the former voyage and, still affluent, he invested elsewhere.

The Elizabethans' appetite for exotic foods, spices and sugar drove the Barbary Company to fulfil demand. William became a founding member among whom were a cultivated family of merchants and owners of property in Marrakesh and the Playa d'Agadir. These were the Gore brothers, Thomas and Gerard Gore. It was within this family that in 1580 William found his wife, Margaret, the daughter of Thomas Gore, famed for his hospitality at St. Stephen's Walbrook, London. Margaret and William had seven children,[vii] three daughters, Anne, Elizabeth and Margaret each married merchant adventurers. Son Gore educated at the Merchant Taylors' school and Gray's Inn, became a lawyer and son William, also educated at the Merchant Taylors' school became apprenticed to Thomas Harvey, brother of the famous Dr William Harvey.

The colourful merchandising activities of Thomas and Gerard Gore, William Bond the younger and their partners, amongst the Jewish community of Morocco and Marrakesh were complex and quarrelsome. This led to speculation about Shakespeare's knowledge of Jewish trade and merchants when he wrote the 'Merchant of Venice.' An article entitled, 'Portia and the Prince of Morocco' argues that Shakespeare knew the Gore brothers and through the difficulties they had experienced in retrieving loans, he had learnt about Jewish trade and culture. The Gore brothers had traded English cloth in return for sugar from the Moroccan Sephardic Jew, Isaac Cabeça, a banker and sugar baron. He is thought to have been the inspiration for Shylock in Shakespeare's *Merchant of Venice*. Cabeça had become bankrupt and imprisoned through his inability to repay a debt of 50,000 ounces of silver to Sultan Abdullah al-Ghalib. The Gore brothers were thus unable to retrieve the thousand pounds owed to them and this led to a hearing in the high court of admiralty in London. After negotiations to release Isaac Cabeça, the Gores and Cabeça helped one another with the financial setback brought about by the sultan's increase of sugar leases. The Gore brothers clearly intended to carry on trading with the Jew, described in the High Court as a '*famous and jolie merchant*.' This view contrasts with the cultural fear towards Jews said to exist within English society.[84]

Many new trading companies were formed around the world in the last years of the sixteenth century and beginning of the seventeenth century, the most famous being the Virginia Company and the East India Company. William Bond the younger joined the new Levant Company. It had merged with the Turkey Company to import spices, raw silk, soft leather, indigo, raisins, coffee and medicinal products from Syria, Egypt and Turkey.

William then became a member of the newly-formed Spanish Company in 1605. It might be considered a venture fraught with difficulty after the recent aggression between Spain and England towards the end of the previous century as experienced by his father, yet those still alive who had suffered loss of cargo, money and vessels, nevertheless, believed it could offer good returns. The two erstwhile antagonists, King Philip II of Spain and Queen Elizabeth I, had passed away and the newly crowned King James I was keen

---

[84] 'Portia and the Prince of Morocco',
https://www.thefreelibrary.com/Portia+and+the+Prince+of+Morocco.-a0108477347

to form an alliance in the hope of lessening Catholic aggression against Protestant England. The London Treaty of 1604 agreed that Spain would recognise Protestant England and the non-restoration of Catholicism. The merchants, no doubt, reasoned that this better understanding would smooth the path of commerce, but William did not live long enough to find out. He died in 1608, aged about fifty-three, and is buried at St. Stephen's Church, Walbrook, London. Spain and England remained at peace for the next fifty years.

The Walbrook area where William Bond the younger and other members of the Bond and Gore families lived is one of the oldest regions of London and was first settled by the Romans with a great fort or legionary camp. For a thousand years a great wall surrounded London, known as Londinium making it one of the safest towns in Europe and ideal for the local and overseas merchants who traded there.

In mediaeval times industry and crafts thrived with mills, millers, tanners and leatherworkers all drawn by the source of power provided by the river, but the ever expanding population eventually led to the Walbrook rivulet being vaulted over with houses. The original church became too small and a new structure was built in the fifteenth century only to be destroyed in 1666 as the Fire of London swept through the City. The new St. Stephen's was designed by Sir Christopher Wren and is described as the most beautiful of the London churches. More recently, when rebuilding the Guildhall Art Gallery, the builders broke through the remains of a Roman amphitheatre and a little further away over forty skulls were discovered with the likelihood that there are many more, all within the perimeter of the wall. In Roman times bodies were buried outwith the town walls, so to whom did these bones belong? Had they been decapitated? One archaeological review says not. Were they gladiators, criminals or the result of headhunters? Were they victims from the defeat of the Boudican revolt in AD60/61? It is thought not. Dating of the skulls and other archaeological evidence indicates that the skulls are from a later period. It is a mystery but the Museum of London and other similar sites lay out the evidence and reasoning for what may have happened and can be found online.

The next chapter refers to the Bond family's cousin. This is Simon Bourman from Devon. His life provides insight from within Spain of the fractious political turbulence between Spain and England that caused so much trouble to the merchants of William Bond and William Whitmore's era that ultimately ended in battle.

Simon Bourman b. ca. 1525/30–1601

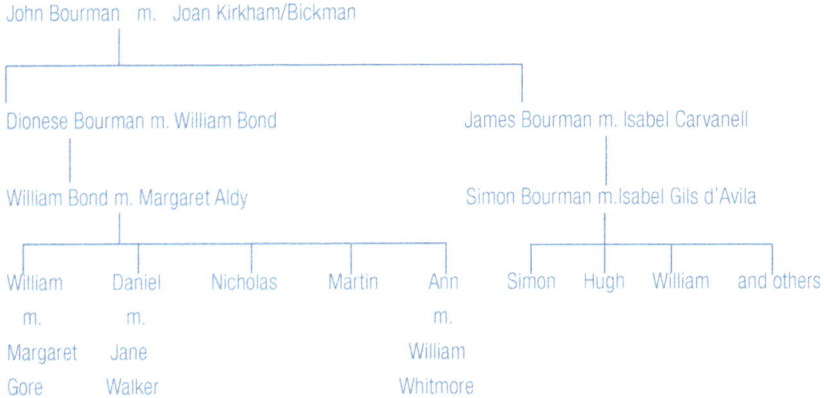

Events during his lifetime

- 1525 Muslims living in Spain ordered to convert to Christianity or leave the kingdom
- 1570 Privateers plunder the richly laden caravels in the Spanish Main on their way home to Europe
- 1587 Francis Drake destroys Spanish vessels in Cadiz
- 1588 Spanish Armada

Anglo–Spanish feuding had created huge suspicion and intrigue in both nations. In Spain all English nationals, whether practising and loyal Catholics or not, came to be regarded with apprehension and distrust. One such person was the Catholic Simon Bourman, his name variously spelt Bowreman, Bowerman, the son of James Bourman of Hemyock, Devon and Isabel Carvanell of Taunton, Somerset. Simon Bourman was also a first cousin of merchant adventurer William Bond the elder .

The Bourman family originated in Brook[85], Isle of Wight but Simon's grandfather, John Bourman moved to Devon and settled in the manor house of Culm Davy, Hemyock, which still exists as part of the present farmhouse. Whereas several of Simon's brothers and sisters remained in Hemyock,

---

[85] 'Parishes: Brook', in *A History of the County of Hampshire: Volume 5*, ed. William Page (London, 1912), pp. 215–217. *British History Online*
http://www.british-history.ac.uk/vch/hants/vol5/pp215–217 [accessed 2 March 2021].

Simon decided on life as a haberdasher, privateer and merchant adventurer.[86] His elder brother, William, lived in Wells, Somerset where he became a member of parliament for the area.

Simon Bourman, operated in Spain in the mid-1550s as one of the best-known English factors in Seville in partnership with his London-based cousin, Sir George Bond, with whom he was a co-owner of the vessel, the *Salomon*. While living in Spain, Simon married a Spanish-born Catholic named Isabel Gyles (Isabel Gils d'Avila),[87] daughter of Stephen Gyles of Malaga and Katherine de la Salde, with whom he had about ten children.

Spanish vehemence against Protestantism reached its apogee in 1576. They feared contamination of their nationals by Protestant beliefs, so when Simon wished to return to England sometime during that year, the Spanish authorities repeatedly refused to allow his wife, Isabel, and son to leave with him. To resolve the matter Simon Bourman sought the help of the English ambassador, Sir John Smith. By the 30 December of that year the ambassador still had not received a reply to his question as to why Isabel and her son could not join her husband.[88] This was the same year that his cousin William Bond, had sought a return of his money detained by the Spanish Inquisition due to Spain's bankruptcy.

Five years rolled by and further delay occurred when the Spanish discovered what they considered to be heretical goings-on in their midst. On 23 July of 1581, Bernardino de Mendoza, a former military commander and now King Philip's spy and ambassador to London, advised King Philip that he had requested the mayor of Province Guipuzcoa to forbid Alderman Bond's ship *Salomon* from loading or taking on any future cargo of coin. Although at least three of the Bonds were aldermen and traded in Spain, the reference is to Sir George, who owned the *Salomon*. The king was also advised that a watch be kept on the ship's movements in other ports. Mendoza also wrote, *'The owners are dreadful heretics and, with the aid of their kinsman, Walsingham, make every possible effort to injure your Majesty.'* But this is not entirely true because Simon Bourman, co-owner of the *Salomon*, was a Catholic. The *Salomon* had already received 40,000 ducats, of which only 6,000 was registered and it

---

[86] Visitations of the County of Somerset in the years 1531and 1575 https://archive.org/details/visitationsofcou00weavrich/page/8/mode/2up

[87] Within the family wills Isabel is referred to as Elizabeth, the English form of Isabel.

[88] 'Simancas: December 1576', in *Calendar of State Papers, Spain (Simancas), Volume 2, 1568–1579*, ed. Martin A S Hume (London, 1894), pp. 534–538. *British History Online* http://www.british-history.ac.uk/cal-state-papers/simancas/vol2/pp534–538 [accessed 2 March 2021].

was expected that the next voyage would carry away a similar amount of currency.[89]

The cause of this situation could have been the shortage of wheat and corn across Europe. With prices rising steeply, King Philip had no alternative but to seek supplies from his adversaries. Bernardino de Mendoza found the help of an English merchant and, on an assurance by the king that the ships and merchants would not suffer embargoes, the merchant agreed that grain would be delivered. That promise was broken. A large outflow of money would seriously embarrass Spain's economy.

However, according to a letter written in August by Mendoza to King Philip, the English were told that the Spanish detainment of English vessels had come about because of Drake's plunder of Spanish vessels and that the Spanish king would not release the merchants' vessels until he received restitution for that plunder. On 7 November, 1581 Bernardino de Mendoza reported to King Philip that Queen Elizabeth was intolerant of such demands and refused the request for restitution. She said the king's actions in Ireland had cost her dear and she was keeping Drake's plunder as recompense. Bribery, blackmail and demands did not work with this queen. She made clear that if the merchants did not receive payment from the Spanish for their stolen property she had sufficient money to pay for it herself.[90]

In October of that year Stelan, the Spanish based agent of Simon Bourman and Sir George Bond, had come to the notice of the Spanish authorities. They had detected that most of the heretical Englishmen who came to Seville stayed at Stelan's house. Bernardino de Mendoza informed the king on 9 October that he had been unable to find out Stelan's religious allegiance, though he was generally acknowledged as a Catholic. Mendoza had evidence, however, that most of those who stayed with Stelan returned to England as Protestants and that these 'heretics' reported that there were many others in Spain who were of Protestant conviction; more than was supposed. Such was the alarm over Protestantism that in a bid to restrict the Catholic population from being infected by these heretics, Mendoza urged King Philip to request

---

[89] 'Simancas: July 1581', in *Calendar of State Papers, Spain (Simancas), Volume 3, 1580–1586*, ed. Martin A S Hume (London, 1896), pp. 139–152. *British History Online* http://www.british-history.ac.uk/cal-state-papers/simancas/vol3/pp139-152 [accessed 2 March 2021].

[90] 'Simancas: November 1581, 1–15', in *Calendar of State Papers, Spain (Simancas), Volume 3, 1580–1586*, ed. Martin A S Hume (London, 1896), pp. 203–219. *British History Online* http://www.british-history.ac.uk/cal-state-papers/simancas/vol3/pp203-219 [accessed 24 May 2021].

the inquisitors in Seville to forbid any stranger from lodging in the house of another stranger.[91]

It was now five years since Simon Bourman had first sought the aid of the British ambassador to Spain to allow his family to join him in England. What had happened regarding the ambassador's negotiations over those years? Not much it seems, for in 1580/81 two sons were born in Spain. Then in 1581 Simon applied for Letters of Denization and Act of Naturalisation for twin sons, Hugh and Simon and his wife named Elizabeth (the English version of Isabel).[92] It would appear, therefore, that Simon had at last been given leave to travel to England and indeed this is confirmed by the 1582 Subsidy Roll for Bishopsgate Ward, which lists him paying £50 in tax, that is approximately £10,000 as calculated in 2017. He was living in the parish of St. Martin Outwich, London, which bordered Bishopsgate.

According to the Simanca papers, despite all the setbacks after the events of 1581, trade between Spain and England continued, though the political situation between Spain, France and England remained fragile, especially as England was protecting Spain's adversary, the new king of Portugal. Like some kind of chess game the diplomats for each country schemed and plotted, aided by their respective buccaneers.

Once Simon and family had arrived in London, he and Sir George Bond exported and imported a variety of commodities between Spain and England unmolested. Nevertheless, both monarchs remained suspicious of the other's intention and it was not long before trouble flared up once more. In June 1585 goods, which included oil for Sir George Bond and Simon Bourman, and rope for William Bond the younger, had already been loaded onto the London bound vessels *Manwell* and *Gillian*, at the port of St. Lucar. Then, to the horror of their agent Roger Howe, the Spanish confiscated the ships' sails and those of other merchants. They then placed two Spaniards on board each of the detained ships.

The merchants demanded an explanation from both the king's factor and the council in Seville, which was some 100 miles away. They received word that the king had need of the ships, goods and coinage and that they would receive payment when the fleet came in, but to which fleet this refers is not clear. The seizure of the vessels now lying idle in port not only prevented further trade, it also prevented the merchants and crews from returning

---

[91] 'Simancas: October 1581, 1–15', in *Calendar of State Papers, Spain (Simancas), Volume 3, 1580–1586*, ed. Martin A S Hume (London, 1896), pp. 175–185. *British History Online* http://www.british-history.ac.uk/cal-state-papers/simancas/vol3/pp175-185 [accessed 2 March 2021].

[92] Letters of Denization and Acts of Naturalization for Aliens in England, 1509–1603.

home. Finding that no such embargo existed for French ships, the English, Flemish and other affected merchants, all English allies, searched the ports to hitch a lift – a hopeless quest. None could be found. Roger Howe wrote to Alderman Sir George Bond on 15 June 1585 outlining the problem, declaring, *'only the Lord knows what to do as there is no way home.'* Exasperated, his letter expresses the wish that all their goods were out of the country. However, he had still to sell tin and copper for William Bond and he asked Sir George Bond to forward his letter to William Bond and Simon Bourman.

What was the Spanish king's intention? Such harassment did not bode well, and so it proved. The ongoing Spanish hostilities in the Netherlands were a constant cause of disagreement between King Philip and Queen Elizabeth, and that resulted in the Spanish king detaining the English and Flemish fleets and merchants. But that was not all. Roger Howe, like many other merchants, acted as a spy for Walsingham and during his negotiations and discussions with fellow merchants he discovered that there were other occurrences besides the detainment of vessels. In all probability, the Spanish had other more sinister intentions. His letter mentions this concern. He states that the king had amassed 100 ships at Cadiz, another port around the headland, south of San Lucar, and intended to make sail but for what reason he did not know. He also reported that the Spanish were in league with Rome and Venice, the Duke of Savoy and other French noblemen. It was a vital piece of information and it spurred England into action.

During the seizure of the English and allies ships, one vessel did manage to escape. She was the tall ship *Primrose of London*, captained by Mr Foster and previously owned by William Bond but now by John Hawkins, possibly in co-ownership with William's cousin Simon Bourman, whose son is known to have sailed in her. In a surprise attack, several armed Spanish men boarded the vessel with the intention of seizing the ship, crew and captain. The crew, with remarkable presence of mind, grabbed whatever arms were near to hand and in the skirmish killed some of the boarding party, tossed others into the sea and sailed for home with prisoners. On her return to England, the *Primrose* brought the news of King Philip's seizure of merchandise, detainment of men and ships and her own heroic escape.[93]

Though cautious, Elizabeth I knew that she had to appear strong. She was well aware of Spain and France's intention to put a Catholic on the

---

[93] The Principal Navigations, Voyages, Traffiques and Discoveries of the ... By Richard Hakluyt

English throne but she was not a woman that would tolerate what amounted to dishonesty by the king of Spain towards her merchants, even though some of her own actions had raised the tension. After a couple of provoking treaties by each nation, the queen ordered an attack on the Spanish colonies on 19 August 1585. Too canny to involve her own navy, in September 1585, she issued letters of marque to her 'Sea Dogs,' Sir Francis Drake and Martin Frobisher. With a flotilla of around twenty-one ships and a crew of between twelve and twenty on each vessel, they set forth to plunder Spanish ports in Spain and America. By the queen's reckoning, her buccaneers plunder would at least fill her coffers and hinder Spain. On that voyage Robert Crosse accompanied Drake as captain of the Bond-owned vessel, the *Barke Bond*. Drake, a man of Devon, was well-known to the Bonds and their Bourman cousins. Drake's godfather, after whom he was named, was the Bourman cousin Francis Russell, second Earl of Bedford. The actions of both realms escalated friction. Trading with Spain became illegal, though some intrepid souls continued nonetheless. They wanted to retrieve the debts owed them.

After Howe's report of a gathering fleet at Cadiz in 1585, the queen and her advisers knew that Spain would soon mount an attack against England. Simon Bourman, had experienced enough unwarranted Spanish aggravation and, thoroughly disillusioned, he helped to finance a retaliatory voyage to Spain by sponsoring the enterprise and paying the expenses for his own ship. He joined Sir Francis Drake, Roger Howe and seventeen other London merchants as their fully armed ships set sail for Spain in March 1587.[94][95] Although William Whitmore is known to have helped impede the Spanish Armada, he is not mentioned among these men.

On reaching Cadiz, Drake's taskforce of men set fire to 100 Spanish ships and cargo, and burnt and plundered several more in St. Vincent. On the return journey to England, at the mouth of the Tagus, they found a worthy prize, the Spanish galleon *San Felipe*. Too good an opportunity to miss, they captured it and its valuable cargo of silk, gold, spices, ivory and much else, all of which would help to offset the cost of fighting the Armada. As agreed in the commission, the participating merchants and their crew received some of the loot. Drake and his men had done

---

[94] *Sir Francis Drakes, Memorable Service Against the Spaniards* by Robert Leng https://archive.org/details/sirfrancisdrakes00lengrich/page/26.
[95] 'Simancas: May 1587', in *Calendar of State Papers, Spain (Simancas), Volume 4, 1587–1603*, ed. Martin A S Hume (London, 1899), pp. 78–92. *British History Online* http://www.british-history.ac.uk/cal-state-papers/simancas/vol4/pp78–92 [accessed 4 March 2021].

considerable damage, giving England valuable preparation time. Not only had the Spanish lost ships but also the valuable, seasoned wood needed for the caskets that preserved their victuals and water. Drake described the incident as 'singeing the king's beard'. He had frustrated rather than vanquished Spanish aggression.

The merchants' knowledge of local politics and Spanish thinking made it possible for Sir Francis Walsingham to create financial pressure on Spain and the pope. William Whitmore helped by facilitating that pressure on the Bank of Genoa, which was handling funds for King Philip.[96] The pope had promised loans to King Philip, but by cornering a large number of bills drawn on Genoese banks, Walsingham had delayed the build-up of resources to equip the Spanish Armada.[97] His spies and overseas merchants had provided the intelligence for what was afoot. The seizure of money plus Drake's attack had dealt a blow to the King of Spain's plans to conquer England, the Albion thorn in his flesh. But not for long.

Meanwhile, in England other members of the family prepared for the inevitable battle but within their midst lay treachery. Two prisoners of war, the Spanish Francisco Valverde, and Pedro Santa Cruz, a Portuguese, had been captured in 1586 and 1587 respectively while carrying merchandise for Spain. Valverde was placed in the safekeeping of the recusant Catholic household of Simon Bourman and Santa Cruz with merchant, James Naunton who, with his partners, had carried out many raids against Spanish ships. The prisoners were told that they would not be set free until the Spanish king agreed to release Englishmen held in Seville. Extraordinarily, these two captives had somehow acquired access to other Catholics.

In a letter of 27 February 1588 to Bernardino de Mendoza, the Spanish ambassador to London, Valverde reported fulsomely on the activities of three English agents, all Jews, based in England and Spain. They were the London-based Portuguese merchant and physician Dr. Hector Nuñez, whose wife subscribed to the secret synagogue in Antwerp, and two members of his family, Geronimo Pardo, in Lisbon, and Bernaldo Luis, based in Madrid, each of whom were furnishing Walsingham with details about Spain's preparations for battle. Valverde and Santa Cruz commented: *'The forces are a mob of riffraff with few leaders more cunning at banquets than war.'* They also provided very comprehensive information on the movement

---

[96] Chastleton House by Margaret Dickins
https://archive.org/details/chastletonhouse00dick/page/12

[97] *A Comparitive Chronology of Money: Monetary History from Ancient Times to the Present Day – 1500–1599.*

of English ships. It seems inconceivable that these two captives could have been present in Dr Nuñez house when he received news about the Spanish ships, their men and stores, or that these prisoners were able to question Nuñez's servant about letters received from the doctor's contacts, yet they did. How was it that Valverde and Santa Cruz could obtain that evidence, and how on earth did Valverde get his letter to Mendoza? There was no question as to Simon Bourman's loyalty to England but he moved among London's elite owing to his privileged position and family connections, which provided a network of contacts at the highest level within the aldermanry, the court and fellow merchants, a godsend to a mole in the camp. Unbeknown to him, the mole was within his household; a home of divided loyalties. Isabel gils d'Avila, his wife, prejudiced and devoted to her native country, had the opportunity to eavesdrop and spy. She also spied on the Marranos (crypto-Jews) in the belief that they conspired against Spain.

Forced into Christianity in Spain, these Sephardic Jews had sought refuge in England and other European or Muslim countries at the end of the fifteenth century. The name Marranos (pigs) was a Spanish slur meaning 'filthy'. In England, the question of Jewishness had not arisen for centuries, which meant that although they did not have all the privileges of the indigenous population, there were no particular sanctions against them. Unfortunately, the travails between England and Spain during the run-up to the Armada induced the ardently Spanish Isabel Bourman to spy on both Jews and Protestants.

The scheming Isabel invited these Jews to her house in the hope of discovering their supposed treachery against Spain, which she planned to pass on to the two prisoners held in the two merchants' homes. Why was Isabel so deceitful? Although the daughter of Stephen Gyles, a Spanish-born English merchant from a Somerset family, she had been brought up in Spain and her mother was Spanish. Isabel's childhood memories, and Spanish family proved stronger than allegiance to her husband and his country.

When Isabel learnt that the prisoners Valverde and Cruz were to be released, she uttered a curse that they suffer a tormented voyage unless they did as she now requested. She demanded that on reaching Spain, they inform the Spanish king of the treachery of Geronimo Pardo, Bernaldo Luis and Dr Hector Nuñez. The prisoners returned to Spain in March 1588, and immediately reported on the three men and named a further five. They also divulged information regarding the number of English ships, their whereabouts, arms and plans. The following chapter describes what happened next.

The Spanish Armada, 1588

The Spanish wife of the merchant Simon Bourman held a strong allegiance to the country of her birth and through treachery and spying Isabel Bourman (d'Avila) aimed to help the Spanish cause against England unaware that Francis Walsingham's impressive network of spies matched those of King Philip II of Spain. Well informed about each other's preparations, there should be no surprises as the rift between England and Spain reached its climax. Within a year, Spain had replenished the Spanish fleet destroyed by Drake and his accomplices. In May 1588, the Spanish Armada set sail. The queen, the families of this history and their kin awaited their fate, knowing the odds were hugely against them once Philip's Armada had gathered up his highly trained soldiers, based in France, and landed them in England. The outcome of the sea battle would be decisive.

To his already remarkable skills, the tireless Walsingham added brilliant military organisation in preparation for the expected battle on land and sea. England and Elizabeth I owed much to a man who never failed them despite suffering the excruciating pain of what might have been renal colic, renal stones or testicular cancer.

Preparations for an invasion gathered pace. Did William Whitmore's sons, now in their early to mid-teens, experience a frisson of excitement and apprehension as they learnt of the plans for the expected battle from their uncles, Sir George Bond, lord mayor of London, and Martin Bond, captain of the London Trained Bands? Would they and their father be required to use the weapons and armour held within their father's armoury?[98] Had the Spanish army invaded, the eldest almost certainly would have been at his father's side.

Among the English fleet were 34 fighting vessels of the English Navy plus 163 armed vessels contributed by the English merchants. The City companies and lord mayor of London provided another 30 armed ships and 2,140 men at an estimate of over £2,000 per month. There were also 30 flyboats, possibly from the Dutch allies. The fleet included the Bond family's ships, the *Barke Bond*, the *Primrose*, the *Salomon*, the *Jonas* and the *Fortune*.[99] However, it should be noted that the names of vessels taking part

---

[98] Described in Will of William Whitmore 1593.
[99] 'Cecil Papers: July 1588', in *Calendar of the Cecil Papers in Hatfield House: Volume 3, 1583–1589* (London, 1889), pp. 332–341. *British History Online* http://www.british-history.ac.uk/cal-cecil-papers/vol3/pp332–341 [accessed 4 March 2021].

differ within the various texts describing the fleet. Among the august captains such as Drake and John Hawkins were lesser known but highly accomplished sailors. Two were now quite elderly: Sir William Winter in his sixties commanded the powerful *Vanguard* and Sir George Beston (Beeston),[100] nearly seventy, in command of the *Dreadnought*. As the Spanish Armada came within sight of Plymouth on 19th July, the townsfolk lit the first of the warning beacons, followed by the others as the vessels rounded the southern coastline.

London householders had orders to keep a light burning above their doors until dawn, thereby denying cover of darkness should the enemy land. The faster and more manoeuvrable vessels from the British fleet fought and impeded the Spanish vessels as they sailed towards Calais to pick up the Spanish soldiers based there. By 24 July, the two fleets were in position ready to engage. Sir George Bond ordered a strict watch and a large supply of leather buckets in case of fire.[101] On his instructions the church bells tolled the alert and parishioners congregated in their churches praying for deliverance and singing a newly composed battle hymn. The gathering menace of Spain had stirred a future English bishop to galvanise the fortitude of the English people with '*A hymn to be sung by all England – women, youthes, clerkes and souldiers*', invoking God's help against the '*mercilesse Envaders.*' He was John Still, the master of Trinity College Cambridge.

> '*Sink deep their potent navies*' and '*their strength and courage break*'. Even if '*cruel Spain and Parma with heathen legions*' broke through, the English would not '*change our Bible*'; if Apollyon himself should come, '*His fiery darts we'll quell.*'[102]

At a later date John Still would become bishop of Bath and Wells, and father-in-law of Jane, youngest daughter of merchant adventurer, William Whitmore.

Meanwhile on shore, under the leadership of the Earl of Leicester, Captain Martin Bond, the youngest son of the late William Bond the elder, prepared his 'army' of men. Though in peacetime he was a haberdasher and merchant adventurer, he had taken on the responsibility for the organisation of the trained bands of London, in readiness for the expected invasion. England, unlike Spain, did not have a regular fighting force or army until seventy years

---

[100] The Naval and Military Magazine Vol. 2, pp 596
[101] London and the Kingdom – Volume I Sharpe, Reginald R. (Reginald Robinson), 1848- Gutenberg Press Refs 1671–1672 in this book: Journal 22, fo. 196b. and -_Id._, fo. 196. https://www.gutenberg.org/ebooks/19800
[102] John Still Oxford Dictionary of National Biography. Date of hymn 1588.

later in 1660. For now, the military might of England lay with each county's trained band, a defence newly formed around 1557 on the order of Elizabeth I to protect the realm. Lord lieutenants had instructions to command and organise the militia of the shires and hold reviews of men, armour and munitions. They also arranged for experienced men to train a member of each household in the use of the pike and musket. Each locality within the counties had to supply trained and armed men. Property owners had to supply at least one man or more. As for payment, this ragtag band of volunteers and compulsory soldiers received no regular recompense for their service, even though some had to sacrifice their usual income.

The trained bands of London were based at Tilbury, the most likely place for Spanish troops to land once they had vanquished the English fleet. Under the command of Martin Bond, their captain, they were the most disciplined of a motley army of freeholders, householders and their sons compelled to join in the defence of the country when called upon to do so; the 'riffraff' described by Valverde, the Spanish prisoner with whom Isabel Bourman had consorted.

Such units had no cohesion or regular training. It was a thankless task. Such was the penury of Elizabethan England that this unpaid army of part-time, novice soldiers had to feed itself. Some resented the imposition, preferring to carry on their usual employment than risk their lives for little reward. Unfit, they were for the most part ill-prepared and ill-equipped against invasion and no match against Europe's finest professional and well-practised army. To make matters worse, the Spanish soldiers were under orders to march to Gloucestershire and destroy the Forest of Dean, the source of England's finest oak used to build her fighting vessels and merchant brigs. But first they had to win the battle at sea.

The Spanish ships in tight, defensive crescent formation lay off the coast of France at Gravelines as they prepared to pick up their soldiers. The English fleet, though superior in number, were dangerously low in ammunition having already expended some during skirmishes against the Spanish vessels as they rounded the English coast. As England's commanders surveyed the 132 well-armed ships of the Spanish flotilla, it must have seemed a daunting foe. Out-gunned, the English had to rely on other skills: the courage of her sailors and the tactical ingenuity of her seasoned and able commanders, something the Spanish lacked. Their leader, the inexperienced Duke de Medina Sidona, was no seaman. He had taken command after the death of the veteran Spanish admiral, Santa Croce. The Spanish vice-admiral, Paliano had also died.

The English admirals came up with the idea of fire ships.[103] The 150-tonne

---

[103] From: *Philip II: King of Spain and Leader of the Counter-Reformation* Google book by David Hilliam.

Barke Bond with seventy guns, captained by William Poole, under Drake, was one of eight ships to be sacrificed. At midnight on 28 July, these vessels, packed with gunpowder, slid silently amid the sleeping galleons. Fire and confusion quickly took hold. For once nature also played a fair hand for England. The winds and tides becalmed the Spanish as they cut anchors to flee the flames. With their fighting configuration in disarray and their vulnerable hulls exposed to broadside cannon-fire, they soon succumbed to the English fleet lying in wait to windward. This much-feared Armada with the capacity to wreak havoc suffered a resounding defeat. Fifty-one ships of the Spanish flotilla were wrecked, two sunk and twenty scuttled. Their dead and wounded numbered 20,000. The English lost not one ship, other than those used as fireboats, and had only 400 casualties.

But one of the greatest and most shocking aspect of this battle was that the English sailors received little reward. Worse still, typhus and dysentery swept through the ships' crews causing serious illness and the death of many. Deserted in their hour of need, Queen Elizabeth refused money to help these courageous men. The treasury was bare and Elizabeth had to seek loans from the livery companies. Instead, the commanders of the fleet did what they could for these sick men using their own resources.

But for a capricious lack of wind and the inexperience of Medina Sidona, the Spanish fleet had appeared invincible despite the ingenuity of the English, yet recent research on an English vessel raised from the seabed off the coast of France has proved that the English fleet did have assets not hitherto realised. The guns of the English naval vessels were far superior in quality to those of the Spanish than had been supposed. Up to this time there had been no equality of type, strength, accuracy or safety among ship cannon, which sometimes back-fired, causing dreadful injuries or worse to the 'powder monkeys'. However, the guns on this raised ship were all identical and had a further refinement. Reconstruction showed they could fire accurately for up to a mile and with such force that the cannon ball could pass right through a vessel. How did this come about? The cannon guns were cast in a single mould rather than being welded together. This made them much stronger, more accurate and far less dangerous to the men and boys stoking the barrels. They could fire very large cannon balls and the guns could not split asunder. In fact, such guns were far ahead of those possessed by any other country, including Spain, and were still in use by Nelson at Trafalgar though by that time the iron master John Wilkinson had added a further refinement to the core, making the guns even more accurate and safe.

So after all, though low in ammunition, the Elizabethan navy did have the wherewithal to be a lethal foe. Further research has also revealed that the

Spanish cannon were of poor quality. Nevertheless, beating the Armada was a close run thing and it had been a costly venture, but success however tenuous, is success.

The time had come for Elizabeth I to capitalise on triumph and impress her realm. She aimed also to hearten the troops, for although the majority of the Spanish fleet had been routed, some vessels were still in the vicinity and remained a potential danger should they attempt to land Spanish soldiers. A fighting spirit might yet be required. She gathered her court and rode to Tilbury. There, on 9 August 1588,[104] as many of the defeated Spanish Armada limped homeward, Elizabeth I (Gloriana) gathered her troops to deliver her famous rousing speech of victory, a speech that glorified her realm, its people and its monarch.

'I know I have the body of a weak and feeble woman, but I have the stomach of a king, and of a king of England too, and I think foul scorn that Parma or Spain or any prince of Europe should dare invade the borders of my realm.'

Elizabeth I, not known for bestowing many favours upon those that served her well, did reward a few men for their valorous acts and one of them was Sir George Beston (Beeston). According to the despatches, Sir George had fought every Spanish ship within range of his guns. The spritely Sir George received his knighthood on the deck of the *Ark Royal* in return for commanding the *Dreadnought*. He died in 1601 in Calais. His memorial at Bunbury Church, Cheshire states he lived to 101/2 making him about 88 at the time of the Armada,[105] but the inquisition held at the time of his death makes it clear he was aged about 82 when he died. Nevertheless, to fight and safeguard his vessel and men at the age of seventy-eight is an undoubted achievement, particularly in an age when so many things were more difficult and arduous than today. Mishaps and physical frailty had to be overcome by robustness of mind and spirit rather than medicine.

Amongst the Armada folklore is the belief that the West Highland terrier descends from dogs that came ashore from the wrecks of Spanish Armada ships off the coast of West Scotland. The 'Westie' type dogs were supposedly

---

[104] Different dates for the sequence of events of the Armada are cited in historical texts. The dates used here are those given by the Royal Museums Greenwich.

[105] Age and date of death from memorial at Bunbury Church, Cheshire. The Monuments at Bunbury Church, Cheshire, Transactions of the Historic Society of Lancashire and Cheshire, Vol. LXX. There is a picture of his memorial with several coats of arms including one which links the Beston (Beeston) family to that of merchant William Whitmore. https://www.hslc.org.uk/wp-content/uploads/2017/06/70-6-Rylands-and-Beazley.pdf

part of the ship's complement having the task of keeping down the rat population. Another animal tradition is that the tail-less Manx cats swam ashore from a wrecked ship, having first come on board the ship in the Far East. The vessel is said to have foundered in the Irish Sea on 'Spanish Rock' off the coast of the Isle of Man. There is, however, no proof of such a ship. The Manx cat is thought to be a genetic mutation. The 'Westie' tale is similarly fictitious. The sixteenth laird of Poltalloch, Colonel Edward Donald Malcolm of Argyll, first bred the 'Westie' in the nineteenth century when he decided he wanted a white terrier.

Whether Simon Bourman ever found out about his wife's treachery or whether their marriage survived, we may never know. However, Isabel was a beneficiary in the 1589 will of Simon's brother, Henry Bourman (Bowreman) of Chard, as well as in the 1591 will of Simon's cousin Sir George Bond. Isabel died in 1599 and Simon in 1601. Simon had evidently remarried but when is not known. His will mentions wife Margaret as well as some of his daughters and sons Hugh and Simon, though apparently none by Margaret. These two sons remained loyal to England but made use of their Spanish descent.

Martin Bond 1558–1643

Events during his lifetime

- 1603 James VI of Scotland becomes James I of England.
- 1616 William Shakespeare dies
- 1625 James I dies and his younger son Charles I becomes King Charles I
- 1642 Start of English Civil War

Martin Bond, the dashing, popular soldier, merchant adventurer and youngest son of William Bond and Margaret Aldy was born in 1558 and is thought to have been educated at St. Alban Hall, Oxford.

At thirty years of age Martin served as chief captain of the trained bands of London during the preparations for the threatened invasion of England by the Spanish Armada. Though defeated, Spanish hostility continued until 1603 when the Scottish king, James VI inherited the English throne as James I of England. While outside threats against the kingdom diminished, internal strife increased. Puritan intolerance towards Anglican and Catholic beliefs caused disruption and when King Charles I acceded to the throne, his intransigence towards Parliament divided the nation. To maintain peace, the continuation of the London Trained Bands became a necessity and Martin remained their commander until his death.

Martin, like his brothers, became a merchant adventurer. Having acquitted himself well as a haberdasher, he was admitted to the livery of the company in 1589 and in 1590 he joined his brother Nicholas in business. Nicholas, operating in Riga in Russia had become one of the most successful of the leading importers of flax from Russia. Together, the brothers began trading in Stade in Lower Saxony. Their German factor, Matthias Hoep, based in Hamburg, received cloth from London, which was then sent on for sale by Martin and Nicholas's agent in Lübeck in return for leather, hemp and flax. The brothers had an enterprising business well set up for the future but then the unexpected happened. Nicholas, a young man in his mid-thirties, died. He was buried, at his request, in the family church of St. Helen's, Bishopsgate, London.[106] Despite this sad loss, the business flourished and by

---

[106] Nicholas Bond was a master haberdasher and had several apprentices during the 1580s. He died ca 1590 and gifted money to his family, the Marshalsea prison for poor debtors, several charitable hospitals for orphans and others in need and three apprentices.

1597 Martin, ahead of his competitors, had acquired a packing press. His success enabled him to invest in the Spanish Company, of which he became a director, the Somers Island Company, and the Virginia Company. He also became the deputy governor of the Irish Society, which saw the development of plantations in Ulster during the reign of King James I.[107]

Tireless and dependable, Martin held a number of civic posts during his long life. His interest in retaining London's historic buildings for posterity led him, in 1606 to become one of the surveyors for the replacement of the crumbling City Aldgate Arch. While searching amongst its foundations, the excavators found a hoard of Roman coins. The Romans had landed in Kent in AD 43, sailed up the Thames and built the Roman port of Londinium. Martin thought it appropriate that a replica carving of two of these coins, which represented the Emperors Trajan and Diocletian, be placed on the outer walls of each side of the completed arch – a fitting reminder of when Britain was part of the Roman Empire. The remaining coins went to the Guildhall.[108] London flourished during the Roman period. Today forums and arenas continue to be found and excavated and a statue of Trajan exists on Tower Hill. He had become emperor of Rome in AD 98 and two years later ordered the withdrawal of Roman troops from Scotland. The Croatian-born Diocletian reigned as emperor 200 years later from AD 284. After the Romans left Britain around AD 410 leaving behind developments in agriculture, urban planning, mining of iron ore and constructions, including the Fosse Way, Roman baths and the Hadrian and Antonine Walls, the English began to forget their Roman inheritance and fell back into their former primitive state.

It is thought provoking to consider that thirty-six years after the Romans landed in England, Vesuvius erupted in AD 79 and Pompeii lay under ash until discovered nearly 2,000 years later. The fifteenth and sixteenth-century citizens of over-crowded London would have been amazed had they known of the municipal advantages, cleanliness and comfort of the average Pompeiian.

Above the City Aldgate arch an inscription reads:

'Senatus populusque Londinensis

1609

Humphrey Weld, Mayor'

---

[107] History of Parliament online – Martin Bond 1558–1543
https://www.historyofparliamentonline.org/volume/1604–1629/member/bond-martin-1558–1643 accessed March 2021.
[108] John Strype's survey.

Sir Humphrey Weld, lord mayor of London that year was the father-in-law of Frances, a daughter of merchant adventurer, William Whitmore and Martin's niece. As the centuries rolled by so did the increase in London's traffic. By the eighteenth century, Aldgate Arch had become an obstruction to the flow of traffic and the City of London ordered its removal. Not wanting to destroy the arch, a Mr Mussel used it for his newly built home in Bethnal Green.

Over a period of thirty years Martin Bond worked prodigiously. As a member of the Common Council, he oversaw the preparations for the visit to London in 1606 of the king of Denmark, brother-in-law of King James I. Three years later, he acted as a London auditor until 1611 and again from 1623–1625. In recognition of his financial expertise, he was appointed as auditor and then treasurer of St. Bartholomew's Hospital 1617 to 1642 having been appointed governor of the hospital in 1607. St. Bartholomew is London's oldest hospital, founded in 1144. It was here, during Martin's tenure, that the physician William Harvey discovered how the heart pumped and circulated the blood through the vascular system of the body.

In 1616 the City of London's aldermen elected Martin to the first presidency of the Honourable Artillery Company and at that time the first set of rules and orders were printed. Established by Henry VIII in 1537, the Honourable Artillery Company is the oldest regiment of the British Army. The regiment played an essential role in the defence of the City and acted as a bodyguard for the lord mayor of London when on official business. It also fought on both the Royalist and the Parliamentary sides during the English Civil War. Col. Martin Bond had responsibility for choosing officials, the financial affairs of the company and the training and exercise of the soldiers. As if all this was not enough, Martin represented London as an MP in the Parliaments of 1624 and 1625, and with Sir Thomas Middleton, Sir Heneage Finch and Robert Bateman, he defended the monopoly of the merchant adventurers against criticisms of the outports. In theory, the trading companies were national ventures open to anyone but were, in fact, run by a small number of wealthy merchants who guarded their monopoly rights. In Parliament at the same time were Martin's cousin Thomas Bond and nephew, Sir William Whitmore and Richard Daniell. 1624 was an eventful year as Martin had also been elected as an alderman and master of the Haberdashers' Company.

The Bond family certainly had a gift for working hard and making money but they also had an altruistic outlook. As a trustee of the Haberdashers Company, Martin Bond bought and conveyed Hatcham Barnes to the William Jones Haberdasher School in Monmouth. It formed part of the Jones

Monmouth Charity and still provides income for the Monmouth School for Girls, Jones' Grammar School and West Monmouthshire School at Pontypool. With his nephew, Sir George Whitmore, Martin bought the wardship of their ten-year-old nephew, the future gallant soldier Lord William Craven, son of Sir George Whitmore's sister, Lady Elizabeth Craven, thus keeping it within the family and thereby protecting Craven's inheritance during his minority. In the usual tradition of money lending by the wealthy in the absence of banks, Martin acted as a money lender to several people including Sir Thomas Hardres of Hardres Court, Kent, whom he may have known through his mother's Kentish family. Like many others appalled by King James I delay in providing help to his daughter, Elizabeth, known as the Winter Queen and wife of the elector, Frederick V, Martin contributed to the Palatine Benevolence. The king's dilatory concern was, however, in response to several political considerations.

Martin Bond, who had always acted in the best interest of his country and fellowman, found that others were less than amiable where religion was concerned. He became innocently embroiled in Puritan and Laudian rivalry at his church, St Katherine Cree. He and his fellow parishioners clashed with the Puritan perpetual curate, Stephen Denison. Magdalene College, Cambridge owned the living, which was leased to some of the parishioners who appointed the cleric. Denison had no intention of compromising his strong Puritan convictions in order to curry favour with the wealthy payers of his somewhat meagre stipend. This, and his abrasive preaching did little to enhance his relationship with these parishioners. When, supported by Bishop Laud, the parishioners requested a select vestry rather than a general vestry, they felt the full force of Denison's vituperation and denouncement from the pulpit.

That was not the least of these parishioners' offences in this clergyman's opinion. The rebuilding and repair of the church also invited his opprobrium. Martin Bond had been involved in the rebuilding of the crumbling church for which the City livery companies, East India Company, and court of aldermen gave generous donations. Lord Craven, Martin's great nephew provided funds for the repair of the steeple. Martin laid the first stone and bestowed a service book with silver bosses and clasps for the Communion table. He also commissioned the installation behind the altar of a beautiful, stained glass roundel window, perhaps to represent the Katherine Wheel on which St. Katherine, the patron saint of the church, had been martyred. Such ornamental, Romish extravagance went far beyond the sensibilities of the puritanical Stephen Denison's ideal of plain and unadorned places of worship. Such was his antagonism that Martin and the future lord mayor of London, Sir John Gayer, were unable to enjoy holy rites in the church of their creation and felt compelled to change their place of worship to St. Andrew Undershaft instead.[109] Both churches were within the Aldgate area of London and Throckmorton House where Martin lived.

Rose Window of St. Katherine Cree

The grand old family home of Crosby Place had become too big and costly an encumbrance for the single Martin. His elder brothers Daniel and Nicholas had died and William, his second brother, lived with his own family in the Walbrook area of London where he died in 1608. Martin decided to sell Crosby Place to Sir John Spencer, lord mayor of London, a hard-headed and rich business man, who opposed the marriage of his daughter to Lord Compton. Undeterred, Lord Compton carried off his bride-to-be in a baker's basket.

The life of the industrious and long-lived Martin drew to a close just as civil hostilities came to the fore. King Charles I and Parliament became increasingly disenchanted with each other and the differences between the Puritans and other Protestants more divisive. Martin died on 11 May 1643 aged eighty-five before he could become embroiled in the first years of the English Civil War and the end of the monarchy.[110][111]

---

[109] *Negotiating Power in Early Modern Society: Order, Hierarchy and Subordination in Britain and Ireland* Edited by Michael J. Braddick and John Walter.

[110] Register of St. Helen's of Bishopsgate & Abstracts of Probate Acts in the Prerogative Court of Canterbury.

[111] British National Archives – will for a Martin Bond, Haberdasher dated 7 July 1647 and 7 July 1648.

Through his will, Martin provided for his Whitmore, Bond and Bourman nephews and nieces. Members of the Haberdasher Company, his own and other people's servants, and the poor of the parishes in which he lived and worshiped became beneficiaries. St. Bartholomew Hospital received a pewter inkwell bearing his coat of arms, a house in Leadenhall Street and £50.

Inkstand presented to St. Bartholomew's Hospital by Martin Bond

Martin's epitaph commemorates the high regard in which he had been held for his courage and benevolence to others. His memorial and epitaph at St. Helen's Church, Bishopsgate, placed next to that of his parents William Bond and Margaret Aldy, shows Martin in the armour of the time, sitting by his tent, with a sentry, and another soldier holding his horse. The inscription reads:—

> 'Memoriae Sacrum. Neere this place resteth ye body of ye worthy citizen and soldier Martin Bond, Esquire. Son of William Bond, sheriff and alderman of London. He was captain in the year 1588 at ye camp at Tilbury, and after remained Chief Captain of ye trained bands of the Citty until his death. He was a merchant adventurer, and free of the Company of Haberdashers. He lived to the age of eighty-five years, and dyed in May 1643. His piety, prudence, courage and honesty, have left behind him a never dying monument.'

His translated Latin epitaph reads:

> 'How prudent was this soldier, and how noble his mind, his country and his superior officers knew. How great his piety, how extensive his liberality, the poor can testify, as also the religious and the

pensioners on his bounty. This soldier and citizen, ages cannot produce one out of a thousand to equal, nor is his like remembered. William Bond, Esq.,[112] *has erected this as a memorial of his uncle's worth.'*

The Haberdashers Company renovated father and son's monuments during the nineteenth century.[113] [114]

---

[112] Son of William Bond and Margaret Gore.

[113] 'Memorials of the Institutions: CXIV, St Helen's Bishopsgate with St Martin's Outwich', in *Memorials of the Guild of Merchant Taylors of the Fraternity of St. John the Baptist in the City of London*, ed. C M Clode (London, 1875), pp. 337–344. *British History Online* http://www.british-history.ac.uk/no-series/taylors-guild-london/pp337-344 [accessed 6 March 2021].

[114] There are pictures and the inscriptions in full of the Bond tombs in St. Helen's Bishopsgate, in 'Annals of St. Helen's Bishopsgate' by the Rev. J. E. Cox. Published by Tinsley Bros., 8, Cathering Street. Strand. 1876. A copy is available at the Guildhall Library.

Netherland Merchants

While the first William Bond was trading in France and William Whitmore was importing fine fabrics from Spain, the safety of England and her queen were in jeopardy. The aggression of the Spanish, French and Hansa merchants across Lowland Europe, particularly the Netherlands not only hindered English trade, it determined the cautious political response of Queen Elizabeth I. Fear of both France and Spain's wish to put a Catholic on the Protestant English throne resulted in the antagonism between England and Spain that caused the Spanish Armada.

To provide a deeper explanation and perspective on how events affected members of the family living and trading in the Lowlands prior to the Armada, and to comprehend the family links, it is necessary to retrace the years to about 1560.

A small and powerful group of merchants closely linked by marriage governed merchandising in the Netherlands and Calais. With their knowledge of the political scene in this region, they could report to the English court on developments that might affect the English nation and then act on instructions from the court.

Reginald/Reynold Copcott
1546–1597/8

Antwerp Town Hall, sixteenth century
Licensed under the Creative Commons Attribution-Share Alike 3.0 Unported license.

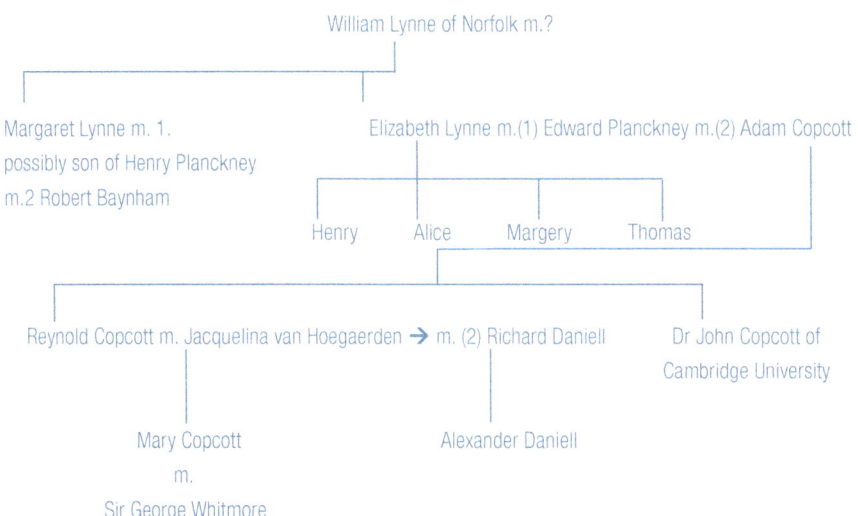

Events during his lifetime

- 1558 England loses Calais to France after 200 years
- 1566–1649 Eighty Years' War between Spain and the Netherlands
- 1568 Revolt of the Netherlands
- 1574 Eighty Years' War – Middelburg declares for the Protestants
- 1576 Sack of Antwerp
- 1579 The Union of Utrecht unifies northern Netherlands
- 1585 Roanoke Island, N. Carolina settled by English colonists
- 1589 Henry of Navarre becomes King of France
- 1590 No trace of first English settlers on Roanoke Island or their settlement
- 1596 Birth of philosopher René Descartes

Spanish domination within the Protestant areas of Northern Europe caused a variety of incidents, which hampered the wool trade in this region over many years. The year 1566 saw a Calvinist revolt against Catholicism and in an event known as the 'Iconoclasm of the Netherlands' the Calvinists destroyed Catholic churches and imagery, prompting King Philip II of Spain to attempt to supress the Calvinists in 1567 – unsuccessfully, as it turned out. A year later the Netherlands rebelled and this marked the beginning of over forty years of intermittent battle with an inevitable disruption to the wool market until 1609. In fact, when added to the later Bourbon–Hapsburg rivalry of 1618–1648, Europe suffered eighty years of recurrent warfare.

Some relief might have been expected in 1576 as Spain's economy fell into serious jeopardy but that brought other problems. Spain then attempted to withhold exports from Spain to England and the money owed to English merchants trading in Spain, as described in earlier chapters. That year Spain declared bankruptcy. Thousands died when the unpaid Spanish soldiers and mercenaries based in the Netherlands sacked Antwerp in the so-called 'Spanish Fury'. As the Netherlands attempted to free herself from Spain's grip, sporadic fighting and pacification continued until Antwerp finally fell to the Spanish nine years later in 1585. Then, another detainment of ships belonging to English and Flemish merchants occurred causing hindrance to the Bond, Bourman and Whitmore members of the Spanish Company. In response, under the Treaty of Nonsuch, 10 August 1585, Robert Dudley, the Earl of Leicester led an unsuccessful expedition on behalf of Queen Elizabeth for the protection of the Protestants partly funded by William Whitmore and Martin Bond, his brother-in-law. At that time Reynold Copcott, then living in Antwerp, transferred his trading activities to other ports. Finally, in 1582 the

Protestant merchant adventurers moved their staple to Middelburg, the Netherland capital of the province of Zeeland, and this is where Reynold Copcott eventually settled.

Unfortunately, information about Reynold is scant since many historical documents held in Belgium and Holland are believed to have perished during World War II, but those that survived and those available within English state papers provide enough to appreciate something of his life and family.

Born into a merchant family sometime between late 1545 and 1553, Reynold had several links amongst the top echelons of merchants within the French staple at Calais, Antwerp, and the aldermen of London. His mother Elizabeth Lynn/Lynne had married at least twice, first to Edward Planckney, who hailed from a Lincolnshire family. Like many of the Planckney family members he worked as a merchant in Calais where he and Elizabeth lived with their four children, Henry, Alice, Thomas and Margery, who would become Reynold's half-siblings. Elizabeth's widowed sister Margaret Baynham also lived in Calais, and after the death of her well-to-do husband, Robert Baynham, mayor of Calais, Margaret carried on his business, trading between Calais and England. She also ran a farm and owned a gabled boarding house, which stood in the market square of Calais. This was where John Johnson of this history had his counting house and where several merchants found a home-from-home during their visits to Calais. Members of the English court had stayed at the boarding house during King Henry VIII's meeting with King Francois I of France at the 'Field of the Cloth of Gold' in 1520, possibly before Margaret married Robert Baynham as his second wife.

Early in 1545 a vicious form of the plague returned to Calais causing several deaths as it had done in England in 1544. Amongst its victims were Reynold's half-sister Margery and John Crant, first husband of Reynold's half-sister, Alice, both then staying with Margaret Baynham. When the plague struck in Calais, Elizabeth Planckney left her shop and the two sisters decided to live in Margaret's garden until it was safe to return home.[115]

Margaret Baynham is reputed to have been a very capable and good-looking woman to whom several merchants were attracted. Good looks may have been an attribute that she shared with her sister because in April 1545 Elizabeth married Calais wool merchant Adam Copcott/Copcote in London. He was her second or possibly third husband. They were the parents of two sons, Reynold and John.

After the fall of Calais to the French in 1558 all English inhabitants had

---

[115] See Letter of Margaret Baynham April 1545. Tudor Family Portrait by Barbara Winchester. London: Alden Press. 1955.

to leave. Adam returned to London and entered the Merchant Taylors' Company. Son, John matriculated at Trinity College, Cambridge in 1562 and Reynold became an apprentice of the Company of Ironmongers around 1567. By 1576 he had become a master of the company followed by admission to the aldermanry and was made a freeman of the City the next year.[116] His father, Adam, meanwhile had become the keeper of the Bayhall in 1576.[117] This was the weekly market for strangers, which permitted foreigners to sell their cloth in London. Although further information on Adam Copcott has not been found, it is possible that he was the son of a John Copcott, a merchant of Calais around 1510. It is known, however, that Adam came from an armorial family because the Copcott arms are incorporated in the shield of his great-grandson, William Whitmore of Balmes, Middlesex.[118]

Of the two brothers, John Copcott, a fellow, and vice chancellor of Cambridge University, a strong defender of the Anglican Church against Puritans and dissenters and chaplain to John Whitgift, archbishop of Canterbury, became the more famous. Reynold, having chosen the lucrative mercantile business in which he excelled, enjoyed a lifestyle of greater comfort than his brother's austere calling.

Ironmongery at that time provided a very good living. There was no shortage of customers for the metal and associated goods imported from Germany, Spain and Normandy. A succession of battles ensured that weapons and armour were much in demand and, in the unlikely event of peace, the need for umpteen household and industrial goods from cooking pots and utensils to a myriad of artisan tools would replace the reduction in weaponry. Reynold, as a merchant adventurer based in Antwerp would have been the source for both metals and implements. He operated in partnership with Fernando Clutterbooke who worked at the London end of the business in Bishopsgate, London. Being a well-respected and likeable man, Reynold became a senior member of the merchant adventurers and quickly rose to become deputy governor of the merchant adventurers of Middelburg, a post that involved him in negotiations and the resolution of

---

[116] Within the apprenticeship records Reynold Copcott is named as Reynold, Capcote. Spelling at this time was fluid.

[117] "The Chamberlain's Account 1584–5: Nos. 1–67', in *Chamber Accounts of the Sixteenth Century*, ed. Betty R Masters (London, 1984), pp. 1–30. *British History Online* http://www.british-history.ac.uk/london-record-soc/vol20/pp1–30 [accessed 7 March 2021]. See Adam Copcote.

[118] The gravestone of William Whitmore within Michaelstowe church in Essex bears his arms. It lies in front of the altar but maybe covered over.

monetary disputes between merchants.[119] He also undertook delicate transactions in Antwerp on behalf of the queen.

Armies need money, the Four Members of Flanders, that is Bruges, the area around Bruges, Ghent and Ypres, were continually short of funds for support of soldiers fighting the Spanish forces. Loans were procured from Queen Elizabeth but that required interest to be paid to the queen when requested. Several areas of the region owed interest but obtaining that interest was far from straightforward.

As Gerhard Prouninck stated to the government of Antwerp in 1581:

'It is impossible to manage a small family well, much less an entire country, especially in times of war, without means of money.'

Hitherto, the very complex religious/political situation in Europe and the Lowlands had demanded care on the part of Elizabeth I. Though implored to take action by Francis Walsingham since 1572, the Queen had refrained from becoming involved in the Lowlands' protests because of the attitude of Catholic France and Spain towards England, which vacillated between friendship and animosity, depending upon whether either country considered religion or trade of greater importance. If religion became the greater issue, then France would very likely support Spain's avowed aim to put a Catholic on the throne of England, namely Mary Queen of Scots, and return England to Catholicism. The Spanish army based just across the Channel in the Netherlands posed a great risk. England, with no formal army, other than the Honourable Artillery Company, formed to safeguard London, had little hope of repelling such a formidable foe, even with the dubious help of the Trained Bands.

Elizabeth also had to consider the consequences to English trade and the economy should the important wool staple suffer disruption. The queen's hesitation seriously worried Sir Francis Walsingham who believed that it was necessary to counteract the Catholic threat. The fervently Protestant Walsingham, then the queen's ambassador to France, and the merchant spy John Bond, a cousin of the merchant adventurer, William Bond had witnessed the horrific slaughter of Protestants during the 1572 St. Bartholomew Day Massacre when many of the Huguenots fled to England. While Bond held a family hostage in order to make his escape, Walsingham had been so deeply shocked by the butchery it shaped his future political

---

[119] 'Cecil Papers: April 1595, 1-15', in *Calendar of the Cecil Papers in Hatfield House: Volume 5, 1594-1595*, ed. R A Roberts (London, 1894), pp. 161-173. *British History Online* http://www.british-history.ac.uk/cal-cecil-papers/vol5/pp161-173 [accessed 21 November 2021]. See Renold Capcot.

belief and actions. He became convinced that Elizabeth should act to protect herself and England yet, despite his entreaties, the queen continued to stall. Instead, she followed the advice of the more cautious Robert Cecil by providing covert loans that would aid the Netherlands in their quest for independence from Spain under the leadership of William of Orange and his son Maurice. Riven by battles, the Netherlands was short of money but so was the queen, and at the end of 1581, when the United Provinces of the Netherlands had gained independence, she requested the full year's payment of the interest owing on her loans.

Walsingham instructed George Gilpin, the secretary of the Merchant Adventurers Company at Middelburg and its representative in Zeeland, to ensure that the Four Members of Flanders repay the interest to the financiers in Antwerp.[120] George Gilpin, turned to his close and trusted friend Reynold Copcott in Antwerp to facilitate this.

However, this was not acceptable to every region. They complained that their situation was such that they could only provide six months of interest. In an effort to resolve the matter, letters continued to pass back and forth between Antwerp and London amid rising tension between George Gilpin and Walsingham. Gilpin felt unfairly blamed for the delay that was not his fault.

Meanwhile, the queen had ordered Gilpin to the diet at Augsberg where he was to negotiate with the Hansa, who aimed to exclude the English from trading in the region. Thus, Reynold Copcott became responsible for carrying out Walsingham's orders on behalf of the absent Gilpin.[121] Toward the end of March 1582 Walsingham tersely reminded Gilpin to leave instructions for Reynold Copcott to act on Gilpin's behalf while he was in Augsberg.[122] Gilpin reassured Walsingham that Reynold was aware of the

---

[120] George Gilpin 1514–1602 was a diplomat, translator and Walsingham agent. Gilpin frequently served as the agent for procuring and repaying Elizabeth's loans in both Germany and the Low Countries during the rest of her reign, and was a paymaster for various diplomatic agents. Besides having substantial financial responsibilities, it is also clear that he was a primary source of intelligence and highly conversant with Dutch affairs. Gin: today we enjoy Gilpin Gin first brought to England by George Gilpin, known as Dutch 'Genever' spirit flavoured with spirits and juniper.

[121] 'Elizabeth: December 1581, 26–31', in *Calendar of State Papers Foreign: Elizabeth, Volume 15, 1581–1582*, ed. Arthur John Butler (London, 1907), pp. 418–437. *British History Online* http://www.british-history.ac.uk/cal-state-papers/foreign/vol15/pp418-437 [accessed 7 March 2021].

[122] 'Elizabeth: March 1582, 21–31', in *Calendar of State Papers Foreign: Elizabeth, Volume 15, 1581–1582*, ed. Arthur John Butler (London, 1907), pp. 571–589. *British History Online* http://www.british-history.ac.uk/cal-state-papers/foreign/vol15/pp571-589 [accessed 5 June 2021].

situation and would act as instructed. Negotiations in Augsberg duly took place and Gilpin impressed upon the Four Members and St. Aldegonde who became burgomaster of Antwerp in 1583 that the situation regarding payment of the interest owing to the queen had to be resolved. Gilpin also advised Walsingham about the health of William of Orange. William of Orange had been shot in the head during an attempted assassination the previous day and Gilpin reported that stemming the bleeding was proving difficult.[123] Nevertheless, the stoic, uncomplaining William the Silent, as he was often named, survived but died two years later in 1584.

Whereas communications were quick and efficient, collecting money owed moved at a very leisurely pace. It was now the end of April. Gilpin and Reynold Copcot set off to Middelsburg on receipt of word that, at last, the interest would be paid to Vander Werke, the pensionary of Middelburg, within six days.[124] Alas, it was not and they were advised of yet another hiatus. Vander Werke told them that although half the interest was available, the other half would not be forthcoming for another twelve–fourteen days and would be less than that agreed at the Hague almost a year before. Gilpin and Reynold stated that this latest development would not be well received by her Majesty and suggested that sorting it out should take priority over any other business and before the states-general disbanded.[125] Ten days duly passed ... and still no money, at which point Gilpin wrote to Walsingham saying that he and Reynold Copcott had remonstrated in person and in writing over a considerable period to no avail and had finally resigned themselves to accept any amount of interest offered.[126]

It would be interesting to know Reynold's views on all of this, other than what is written in the court papers. So far, correspondence between him and

---

[123] 'Elizabeth: April 1582, 6–10', in *Calendar of State Papers Foreign: Elizabeth, Volume 15, 1581–1582*, ed. Arthur John Butler (London, 1907), pp. 612–625. *British History Online*
http://www.british-history.ac.uk/cal-state-papers/foreign/vol15/pp612–625.

[124] 'Elizabeth: April 1582, 26–30', in *Calendar of State Papers Foreign: Elizabeth, Volume 15, 1581–1582*, ed. Arthur John Butler (London, 1907), pp. 657–672. *British History Online*
http://www.british-history.ac.uk/cal-state-papers/foreign/vol15/pp657–672.

[125] 'Elizabeth: May 1582, 1–10', in *Calendar of State Papers Foreign: Elizabeth, Volume 16, May-December 1582*, ed. Arthur John Butler (London, 1909), pp. 1–19. *British History Online*
http://www.british-history.ac.uk/cal-state-papers/foreign/vol16/pp1–19.

[126] 'Elizabeth: May 1582, 11–20', in *Calendar of State Papers Foreign: Elizabeth, Volume 16, May-December 1582*, ed. Arthur John Butler (London, 1909), pp. 20–38. *British History Online*
http://www.british-history.ac.uk/cal-state-papers/foreign/vol16/pp20–38.

Gilpin has not come to light. There are, however, several letters from George Gilpin held within the Cecil Papers at the British Library, also letters from Gilpin to Lord Willoughby at the National Archives. These and letters between Gilpin, Walsingham and Thomas Bodley, a diplomatic envoy working on behalf of Queen Elizabeth I, show how trusted merchants such as Reynold Copcott and Valentine Palmer who had married into the Bond family were used to convey important information to the English court.

As it turned out, loans to the embattled Protestant armies and attempts at negotiation with the Hansa accomplished little. Battles persisted on and off across the Netherlands until 1585 when Antwerp fell to the Spanish causing an exodus of Protestants to Amsterdam.

Walsingham had a number of spies amongst the merchantry and, although not officially a spy, Reynold Copcott supplied intelligence whenever he came across useful evidence. In October 1585 he advised William Davison, Queen Elizabeth's Secretary of worrying information received from another merchant. It seemed to refer to some unstated treachery against the queen and was serious enough to impel Davison to ask Reynold to send the merchant to him so he could learn more. Davison also advised Walsingham on 22 October 1585 that he intended to spare no cost in discovering more.[127] He describes Reynold as a *very honest and discreet merchant of our nation at Middelburg*. This treachery may have related to the Parry or Babington Plots,[128] although, around that time, there were several other Catholic plans to assassinate Elizabeth in favour of the Scottish queen who was beheaded for apparent treachery two years later. Around the same time, discussions took place between diplomats as to the loyalty of St Aldegonde, the burgomaster of Antwerp. Walsingham recognised his past usefulness, but Villiers was a great deal more circumspect as to St. Aldegonde's trustworthiness.[129]

Another four years passed before the future looked more peaceful. The Spanish Armada of 1588 had been vanquished and the combative Spain had

---

[127] 'Elizabeth: October 1585, 21–25', in *Calendar of State Papers Foreign: Elizabeth, Volume 20, September 1585-May 1586*, ed. Sophie Crawford Lomas (London, 1921), pp. 102–120. *British History Online* http://www.british-history.ac.uk/cal-state-papers/foreign/vol20/pp102-120 [accessed 7 March 2021].

[128] Bernardino Mendoza a Spanish ambassador to London and Spanish military commander was implicated in the Babington Plot.

[129] 'Elizabeth: October 1585, 21–25', in *Calendar of State Papers Foreign: Elizabeth, Volume 20, September 1585-May 1586*, ed. Sophie Crawford Lomas (London, 1921), pp. 102–120. *British History Online* http://www.british-history.ac.uk/cal-state-papers/foreign/vol20/pp102-120 [accessed 31 May 2021].

over-committed herself. Nevertheless, it was not long before Spain was at war with France. King Philip of Spain attempted to prevent the Calvinistic Huguenot, Henry of Navarre, from becoming king of France. He failed and, at last, Spanish domination was on the wane.

Spain had lost many ships during the Armada and her plundering of Inca gold and silver brought about economic collapse. Such booty had funded aggressive persecution and empire building but, as ever with economics, there was another side to monetary affairs – abundance is not necessarily helpful. Paradoxically, Spain's spending had increased the money supply of Europe, hitherto based in the Muslim world, and that enabled the other European nations to forge ahead and expand their own domains and trade with other lands. Spain's indulgence and over-supply of money had de-based her own currency, causing inflation.[130]

Despite all the disturbances of trade in the Netherlands, Reynold had managed to make a good living and he had played his own small part in the ending of Spanish aggression in the Netherlands. Sometime around 1594/5 he married a Dutch girl from Antwerp many years younger than himself. She was Jacquelina van Hoegaerden, daughter of Jan van Hoegaerden/ Hoogarden and Maria van Meghen,[131] descended from an ancient family of Brabant. Reynold's fortune would secure the future of his wife whose family had suffered considerable adversity. Maria van Meghen, with other children besides Jacquelina to support, had been widowed in 1576 after her husband Jan was killed in their home by the Spanish during the dreadful slaughter in the Sack of Antwerp (Spanish Fury). It was the worst massacre in Belgian history; three days of killing and pillage, in which thousands died. Somehow, Maria van Meghen and Jacquelina, then a small child, escaped with other members of the family, Clara, Baptista and Abraham van Hoegaerden, who were probably Jacquelina's siblings.

Unfortunately, as so often happened in those times of diseases for which there were no cures, the union between Reynold and Jacqueline was brief. The fifty year old Reynold died in Zeeland around 1597/8[132] when his only child, Mary, was about two years old. The many bequests of his detailed and carefully crafted will and his standing within the merchant community and the Company of Ironmongers are proof of his ability, success and his concern for the welfare of his family and friends. His will provided many gifts to family, friends, merchants, servants, the Merchant Adventurers Company and Cambridge colleges once attended by his brother, John Copcott. He

---

[130] Money by Niall Ferguson.

[131] Diary of Alexander Daniell

[132] Will undated. Dates surmised from Richard Daniell's marriage, birth of Alexander and Alexander's diary.

requested that his cousins, Christopher Hampton and Francis Hampton be the guardians of daughter Mary in the event of her mother's death. His fellow merchant adventurers and friends, Thomas Bull and Richard Daniell/Danyell, were to assume guardianship of Mary's financial inheritance if Jacquelina died before Mary reached adulthood.[133] Reynold had been anxious to cover any circumstances that may befall his wife and daughter. He also requested that Mary be naturalised as an English subject to ensure her full rights under English law. Among his wife's family he mentions Abraham, Clara (sister-in-law) and Baptista van Hoegaerden/Hoogarden and his cousins Thomas Crante, Daniel Planckney, and brother Henry Planckney. His half-sister Alice Hampton (Planckney) had died as had brother John. Probate was not granted in London until 13 June 1608 but that is a story for the next chapter.

---

[133] *British Library 171. EDMONDES PAPERS. Vol. VI. (ff. 387).* 28 March, 1609 – 24 March, 1610[1]. p. 116 – Sir Thomas Edmondes to Mr Cullymore, 1609, 9 August, Brussels.

Richard Daniell 1561–1630

Middelburg, Zeeland

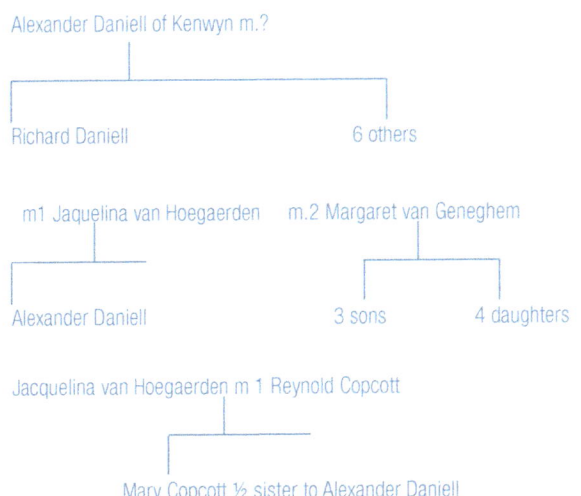

Events during his lifetime

- 1561 Sir Francis Bacon born in London
- 1593 Galileo invents thermometer
- 1600 English physician names electricity electrica
- 1610 Galileo observes moons of Jupiter and spots on sun
- 1625 Charles I becomes King and marries Henrietta Maria
- 1630 John Winthrop becomes governor of Massachusetts Bay Company

Richard Daniell, a Cornishman descended from a family long resident in that county was born in Truro on 5 October 1561 during the reign of Elizabeth I. He was the seventh son of Alexander Daniell of Kenwyn. Cornwall was well positioned for trade with the Netherlands and in 1584, at the age of twenty-three, after an apprenticeship with the Drapers' Company in London, Richard began trading with the Dutch. As already described, the Netherlands was a nation in turmoil; over-taxed, suffering aggression against its Protestant citizens and interference with its trade. The Netherlands had risen in revolt against the overbearing ruling Catholic Spain. Many Protestants had fled northwards to Zeeland and Utrecht in the United Provinces of Holland, which became independent in 1581 after the Dutch Revolt led by William of Orange.

Twenty-year old Prince Maurice of Orange, the head of the Dutch Army, became governor-general of Holland, Zeeland and Frise after the death of his father William, Prince of Orange in 1584. At last, with the United Provinces free of Spanish oppression and the English staple moved to Middelburg in Zeeland, Richard must have thought now was the time to establish a base there, and on 8 March 1586, he set forth for Walcheren, an island of the Zeeland province. By 1590 he had settled in North Street, Middelburg, the capital of Walcheren at the residence of Reynold Copcott.[134][135] It was here, in this ancient city, similar to Amsterdam, that Richard Daniell spent the majority of his working life. Today, thanks to a reconstruction programme, a replica of the old city has arisen from the

---

[134] History of Parliament online : Members 1604–1629, Richard Daniell
https://www.historyofparliamentonline.org/volume/1604–1629/member/daniel-richard-1561–1630.

[135] In the seventeenth century Middelburg was also the centre of the Dutch East India Company through which thousands of African slaves were transported from the city to North and South America.

dust of buildings pulverised during the German raids of 1940. Once more large, gabled mansions and storehouses line the canals just as they had in the sixteenth and seventeenth centuries, standing as reminders of its trading history and the rich merchants of the past. Unfortunately, most of the historical records did not survive.

Following the death of Reynold Copcott, around 1598 Richard entered into partnership with two young London haberdashers, Sir George Whitmore and his agent Henry Polstead (Polstede). They traded in silk, taffeta and other fine fabric through the Company of Merchant Adventurers. At thirty-eight years of age and prospering, Richard was in a position to marry and fulfil Reynold Copcott's last wish regarding his daughter, Mary. Richard became more than a fellow guardian of Mary's inheritance; he became her step-father when, on 13 February 1599, he married Reynold's young widow, Jacquelina. Yet, in this act, he could not have guessed at the discord that lay ahead, or what the future held for Mary. This must have been a love match because by marrying a stranger Richard lost his status and privileges as a merchant adventurer. He, nevertheless, continued to be popular and successful and obtained reinstatement as an adventurer in 1611.

At the end of 1599 on 12 December Jacquelina bore Richard a son, Alexander[136] a half-brother to Mary, but two years later in November 1601 she succumbed to a 'burning fever' and was buried in the Old Church of Middelburg (St. Peter's Church), now demolished.[137] The origin of this fever can only be guessed since it has never been identified. Many diseases cause high fever but they are usually identified by coexisting symptoms. In the 'burning fever' that occurred in England and other European countries from time-to-time, other defining symptoms are, unfortunately, not described. It could not have been the same as the sweating sickness, a disease so virulent people could be dead within two hours of the onset of symptoms. The last recorded case was in 1551 as mentioned earlier in this history.[138] Nor is it likely to have been rye bread contaminated with the ergot fungus: a trigger for painful and grotesque endemic outbreaks, which cause a number of symptoms including a burning sensation as the extremities necrotise. Alexander's diary would surely have mentioned these symptoms. The most likely candidates for the burning ague are typhoid fever or malaria, diseases prevalent in many low-lying, damp areas. At that time both were causes of

---

[136] Named after his grandfather, Alexander Daniell of Kenwyn, Cornwall.

[137] Alexander Daniel's diary.

[138] As described earlier, Otwell Johnson and Henry Southwick died of the Sweating Sickness in 1551, a disease caused by an unknown agent, though there are some indications that it may have been hantavirus pulmonary syndrome.

many deaths throughout England and Europe. Today neither is usually fatal for the otherwise healthy and well-nourished if treated, with the exception of malignant malaria. After Jacquelina's death the two motherless children were sent into the care of their maternal grandmother, Maria van Meghen. Maria van Meghen's will indicates that she owned property within the Brabant area of Antwerp, making it likely that this was where they all lived at that time. Richard did not remarry for another seven years, perhaps an indication of the intensity of his grief or work.

A year or so passed, then on 7 March 1602 Sir Robert Cecil received a letter from J. Wheeler, secretary to the English merchant adventurers at Middelburg.[139] This stated that Richard Daniell had received orders from the Privy Council to return to England *'with a young maid, six years of age or thereabouts, daughter of Reinold Copcott, English merchant, late deceased.'* This letter reported that friends of the girl's mother would not suffer Richard or anyone else to take her to England lest she come under the influence of the Hamptons whom they claimed were not fit guardians, but why?[140]

The terms of Reynold Copcott's will were quite clear as to guardianship. Mary was to remain with her mother but in the event of her mother's death, his cousins Christopher and Francis Hampton were to be guardians of her person, and the merchant adventurers, which included Richard Daniell, to be responsible for a portion of Mary's inheritance. Reynold did not foresee that Richard Daniell would become Mary's stepfather. Were the Hamptons now claiming possession of Mary against the wishes of her grandmother who wished to continue caring for her grandchildren and keep the two children together for as long as possible? Her father's cousins (technically nephews), were among Mary's closest relatives on her father's side and they were entitled to claim Mary under the terms of her father's will. But this case was not straightforward because by marrying Mary's mother, Richard Daniell had become Mary's step-father, and in this case guardianship could mean

---

[139] Wheeler's duties were to promote English trade with the Continent. See Holtgen, Karl Josef (U. Erlangen-Numberg) Trade and Politics: John Wheeler (1560–1617), Secretary of the Merchant Adventurers at Middelburg and Author of A Treatise of Commerce (1601) and DNB.

[140] 'Cecil Papers: March 1603, 1–15', in *Calendar of the Cecil Papers in Hatfield House: Volume 12, 1602–1603*, ed. R A Roberts (London, 1910), pp. 660–676. *British History Online* http://www.british-history.ac.uk/cal-cecil-papers/vol12/pp660–676 [accessed 8 March 2021]. History of Parliament suggests that the Dutch family opposed an arranged early marriage with Sir George Whitmore but makes no mention of the Cecil Papers. Parliament researchers admit that their research only relates to matters affecting Parliamentary history, not the personal lives of MPs, and that they know nothing of the Hamptons.

overseeing welfare.[141] It could also be argued that Reynold's half-brother Henry Planckney was Mary's closest relative on her father side, rather than his nephews, but Henry was much older. In fact, Mary's grandmother was Mary's closest blood relative but, in this era the male line had more rights over a child than the womenfolk.

In 1603 Richard Daniell had applied for naturalisation of his son Alexander and stepdaughter Mary, and this was granted through a bill in the House of Commons and act of the House of Lords in 1604.[142] This did not imply that Richard intended to leave Middelburg with the children at this time, merely that he was protecting the children's future interest with regard to the laws of citizenship that related to those born outside England. He was also adhering to Reynold's wish that his daughter be naturalised. Considered aliens, those born outside the realm were not entitled to the rights of inheritance enjoyed by English people born within England, nor were they permitted to own land. Proving their allegiance and religion was another necessity. Naturalisation, however, was complex and costly, usually afforded only by the wealthy. All the children of this history born and living outside the kingdom were naturalised: another clue to the success of their fathers and the fortunes they had amassed.

Wrangling over Mary's guardianship became a cause of protracted negotiations from 1602 onwards. In the meantime, over the next few years Richard, confident and able, honed his trading skills and acted as an intermediary between London and the Dutch ports of Amsterdam, Rotterdam, Haarlem and elsewhere. Like all merchants of this era, he was at ease with the written and spoken languages required. While negotiations continued regarding Mary's return to England, Richard had married again in 1608, this time to Margaret van Geneghen, by whom he had several children, but this marriage apparently created discord.[143] The diary of his son Alexander records his sorrow at the event. Maybe this was just a case of resenting someone daring to replace their mother. Whatever the reason for Mary and Alexander's dislike of their step-mother, it was a situation that remained unresolved for Alexander and would cause some conflict during his teenage years.

---

[141] Roman Law of Guardianship in England 1300–1600. Richard M. Helmholz.

[142] *House of Lords Journal Volume 2 Note of bills* 'House of Lords Journal Volume 2: Note of bills', in *Journal of the House of Lords: Volume 2, 1578–1614* (London, 1767–1830), pp. 352–354. *British History Online* http://www.british-history.ac.uk/lords-jrnl/vol2/pp352-354 [accessed 8 March 2021]

[143] Daughter of Peter van Geneghen at Dordrecht.

By 1609–10 discussions concerning Mary were coming to a head. On 20 April Francis Collimore, one of the objectors, wrote a letter to William Trumbull, senior secretary at the embassy in Brussels, seeking help on behalf of a cousin regarding Mary Copcott.[144] Collimore stated that Mary was happy in Antwerp, that the family and grandmother were concerned only for Mary's best interests and that they had no objection to her going to England once she had reached the age of discretion.[145] A number of letters then passed between four individuals, namely William Trumbull; Sir Thomas Edmondes, the ambassador to Brussels; Robert Cecil, the lord treasurer; and Lionel Wake a merchant of Brabant, the outcome of which was that by May of that year the ambassador agreed that Mary was to be handed over to Richard Daniell. He also asked William Trumbull to inform the family. Perhaps the Dutch family continued to prevaricate because in August the ambassador wrote to Collimore advising him that the state expected him to comply with the request to hand Mary over to her step-father as promised. The other executors of the will were in agreement with this.[146] So what was going on between the families and why? We can only hazard a guess.

Religious bias might be considered a possible cause for disagreement given that the Flemish Francis Collymore (Collimore) was a Catholic merchant and related to Mary through her Dutch grandparents, but there is no hint of religious bias. The fact that Mary's mother, Jacquelina van Hoegaerden, had married two Protestant merchants and the Spanish had killed Jacquelina's father implies that the Dutch family were Protestant. Besides this, the lives of the merchants show they were pragmatic and that good trading affiliations and kinship were of more importance than religious intolerance. Reynold Copcott's will upholds that view since he names the Catholics, Francis and Robert Collimore, as beneficiaries in his will as well as the ardently Protestant Hampton family.

Who were the Hamptons/Hamptones? They were Reynold's nephews through the third marriage of his half-sister Alice Planckney to merchant adventurer John Hampton, so quite distant relations. But why were they considered unfit? It is a mystery because no documentary evidence has been found to provide enlightenment. It seems Mary's Dutch family considered

---

[144] Collimore's letter to William Trumbull, dated 20 April 1609 indicates that he is acting on behalf of a cousin. Downshire Manuscripts, RR10/59/CFH/jh, p 91.
[145] *British Library 171. EDMONDES PAPERS. Vol. VI. (ff. 387). 28 March, 1609 p. 91 – Francis Collimoer to William Trumbull, 1609, 20 April, Antwerp.*
[146] *British Library, EDMONDES PAPERS. Vol. VI. (ff. 387). 28 March, 1609 pp. 96–7 – Sir Thomas Edmondes to William Trumbull, 1609, 10 May, Brussels p. 116 – Sir Thomas Edmondes to Mr Cullymore, 1609, 9 August, Brussels. p. 229 – Lyonell Wake to William Trumbull, 1609–10, 12 Feb, Antwerp.*

her happiness of paramount importance. Mary had lived in the Netherlands all her life and her adult life makes clear her closeness to her Dutch family and half-brother, Alexander. Added to this, it seems unlikely that she would ever have met the Hamptons. Removing her from the family she knew and loved was not in her best interests. Mary, herself, may have expressed unhappiness. The Dutch family were, after all, her blood relatives and nearest kin. Christopher Hampton, on the other hand, although an honourable man, was a remote figure, unmarried and a career oriented cleric, hardly a good replacement for Mary's grandmother. Christopher Hampton became the Protestant archbishop of Armagh and vice chancellor of Dublin University, and when he left England for Ireland he took his brother Francis with him.

As for Richard Daniell, he had been happy for his son and stepdaughter to live with their maternal grandmother, so was he really anxious to wrest Mary from the family she knew? Had Reynold Copcott known that his young widow would marry his fellow merchant his instructions regarding his daughter might have been different.

In the autumn of 1609 when Mary was around thirteen/fourteen years old, Richard had no alternative but to accede to the command to return Mary to England. He took Alexander with him, probably to meet his uncle T.B. Jenken Daniell, a future mayor of Truro, with whom Alexander was to live while he attended the local grammar school in Truro. The three of them boarded a vessel to cross the English Channel. It was a voyage that turned out to be rather more exciting than they might have anticipated or wished. As their ship came within sight of the Kent coast, the vessel came close to being shipwrecked. The reason for this is unknown but the Kent coastline has treacherous, unseen and, at that time, possibly unchartered sandbanks that shift with the current. Over the centuries, many a ship had come to grief. At exceptionally low tide their bleached wood and rusted skeletons are all that remain of these old victims of the sea and sands.

Where and with whom Mary stayed on arrival in London is not known. Alexander's letters indicate that Mary was to be married but the marriage did not take place for another two years when Mary was around fifteen-sixteen years of age. Her suitor was Richard Daniell's fellow merchant Sir George Whitmore who had resolved many years before that the enchanting child he met should one day become his wife. Unlike, the Hamptons, Mary had known Sir George most of her life. Apart from difference in age, not unusual in this era, this was a good match. They were both wealthy, Mary's inheritance would be safe with the principled Sir George and the marriage would strengthen the partnership between the two merchants Whitmore and Daniell. George and Mary were married on 13 August 1611 at St. John's Church, Hackney,

Middlesex. Sir George was a kindly, very popular and jovial man and theirs was a happy marriage. Over the reigns of two kings, James I and Charles I, their convivial and welcoming household was filled with children, relations and friends. George and Mary entertained many civic dignitaries and hosted the entourage of King Charles I on his return from Scotland.

Richard returned to Holland, and continued with his business in Friesland. He had become conversant with the politics of local government and his aptitude earned him the posts of Deputy Mayor of Middelburg and Deputy Governor of the Company of Merchant Adventurers in that city, the same position held by his erstwhile partner Reynold Copcott. This happy state would soon be disrupted.[147] In 1614, with the misguided advice of Alderman William Cockayne, King James I dissolved the Merchant Adventurers Company in favour of the less successful King's Merchant Adventurers. At this point Richard returned home to Penzance but before leaving he was honoured by the state of Zeeland with the gift of a double gilt and covered standing cup, engraved with the arms of Middelburg. On his return to England the Drapers' Company named him as a liveryman on account of his discretion and sufficiency.

The King's Merchant Adventurers Society ultimately failed and the original society, the Merchant Adventurers of London, was reinstated in 1617, but Richard did not return to the Netherlands. Instead, he traded from his base in Cornwall.

Richard's son, Alexander, now seventeen years of age, matriculated as a fellow-commoner at Lincoln College Oxford on 21 November 1617. Intelligent though he was, he was not the first student to find freedom intoxicating and more fun than study. Much to his father's annoyance, spending his parent's money proved of more interest than the rigours of learning. Alexander refuted this. According to him, the monetary disagreements were the result of malicious intent on the part of his detested step-mother. In his diary he claimed that he was kept short of money on account of this. His father, not convinced, wisely decided that if Alexander would not study then he had to work, and removed him from Oxford a year later.[148]

Perhaps, like many teenagers, Alexander was seeing things from his own point of view, rather than the reality of living according to his means. His step-mother, rather than malicious probably realised the need to conserve the family's money, there were, after all, several other younger children to support. Claiming to be kept unfairly short of funds and annoyed that Richard and his wife with so many children lived beyond their means,

---

[147] Cornwall Archives – Alexander Daniell 1599–1668.
[148] Autobiography of Alexander Daniell by Peter Pool. https://peterpool.co.uk/wp-content/uploads/2020/03/Daniel-Alexander-1599–1668.pdf

Alexander was not above asking his brother-in-law Sir George Whitmore for financial assistance.

During 1620 Alexander accompanied his father on business trips to the Netherlands, including one when he and his half-brother Richard accompanied their father to Dordrecht to settle the affairs of their father's mother-in-law by his second wife. They remained there for eight months, a stay that was not without drama. During a game of cards, some disagreement arose between Alexander and a relation of his step-mother during which Alexander was stabbed. Fortunately, Alexander was not badly hurt and was able to take advantage of this visit to Europe to see his beloved grandmother, Maria van Meghen, in Brabant, a distance of about 80 km.

Evidently, Alexander had either redeemed himself or persuaded his father that stories of his profligacy were untrue or exaggerated, because later that year he went on to study at Leiden University with his father's blessing and proved his worth. Alexander Daniell became a successful merchant like his father. He also became a well-known diarist[149][150] and a prolific writer of 300 letters, amongst which were those to his Whitmore nephews, William and George, the sons of his half-sister Mary.

As the years progressed, Richard turned his administrative and civic skills to local and national politics. He became first a burgess for Penzance[151] and mayor of Truro in 1622. As mayor he became involved in a dispute with Plymouth regarding contributions for an expedition against Algerine pirates. These pirates wrought havoc on the fishing fleets and coastal regions of south-west England for much of the sixteenth and seventeenth centuries. They raided villages, stole hundreds of vessels and sold the crews into slavery. Each year during the final concert of the Henry Wood Proms at the Albert Hall, we sing how *'Britons never, never, never shall be slaves,'* but they were. Over those two centuries it has been estimated that hundreds of thousands were enslaved and endured great cruelty at the hands of these pirates and the Barbary masters. Samuel Pepys encountered two men who had been taken into slavery and he provides a graphic account in his diary of 8 February 1661. *"how they eat nothing but bread and water. At their redemption they pay so much for the water they drink at the public fountaynes, during their being slaves. How they are beat upon the soles of their feet and bellies at the liberty of their padron. How they are all,*

---

[149] Oxford Dictionary of National Biography Alexander Daniel www.oxforddnb.com
[150] Family Coucher Book, Alexander Daniel, of Alverton, 1599–1668. Includes 300 letters to cousins William and Charles Whitmore. As sons of Sir George Whitmore, they were, in fact, Alexander's nephews by marriage.
[151] Penzance: The Biography By Mike Sagar-Fenton

at night, called into their master's Bagnard; and there they lie. How the poorest men do use their slaves best."[152]

A few years later Richard became an MP for Truro in the Parliaments of 1624 and 1628. Among his fellow MPs were Sir William Whitmore, brother of Mary's husband, Sir George Whitmore and the young Oliver Cromwell. Richard at sixty-nine years of age was now quite elderly. On 11 February,1630, after a full and active life beginning during the reign of Elizabeth I and ending in that of Charles I, he died unexpectedly in his sleep apparently from a heart condition at the Manor of Alverton. This had been sold to him by the Whitmore brothers Sir George and Thomas many years before.[153] He had complained that night of the tightness of his doublet. Richard was buried in the chancel of Kenwyn church.

Although a very able and popular merchant, city dignitary and MP, Richard was not as affluent as might be expected. His successful mercantile work in Holland had been disrupted by the formation of the less successful King's Adventurers. His large second family had strained his income just as son Alexander thought, and then Richard's brother Jenken had been unable to repay a considerable loan, although some sources report him as wealthy. Richard's parliamentary years were interrupted when he had to seek permission for leave of absence on receiving the news that his house had burnt down. Much to his relief, the damage was not as great as expected but it caused him to sell off land that would have provided income.

Alexander and Mary's maternal grandmother, Maria van Meghen, lived on in Brabant until her death in 1626 at the grand old age of ninety-six, whereupon Alexander inherited her property, which he sold in 1634 to his cousin Justus Collimore, a merchant of Antwerp. Justus Collimore is likely to have been a relation of Francis Collimore, involved in the quibbling over Mary's guardianship. A firm Royalist, Justus Collimore became involved in the pawning of valuable artefacts, including paintings by Rubens and van Dyke on behalf of the duke of Buckingham, which he stored in his house in Antwerp during the English Civil War.[154]

The lives of these seven closely connected merchants are just a few of the many merchants of their time with an interesting history, some of whom were also related to those described here though more remotely. The Epilogue provides a brief synopsis of the lives of the next generation.

---

[152] Pepys Diary https://www.pepysdiary.com/diary/1661/02/
[153] Cornish People in Cornish Books V.1 But Alexander Daniell's Diary states he died in Truro. The manor included many of the settlements of Newlyn, Mousehole and G.
[154] Literatures of Exile in the English Revolution and its Aftermath, 1640–1690, Ed by Philip Major.

Epilogue

The intrepid adventurers of the 16thC braved the seas to explore and invest in unknown regions of this world, not knowing what they would encounter – strange beasts, the 'edge of the world', icebergs and waves that towered over their vessels. To see replicas of such small ships is to wonder how they achieved what they did and marvel at the courage of the sailors and investors. They did not even know the geography of the lands they sought or have reliable navigation instruments with which to find their way.

Five hundred years have passed since then, and the same questing spirit of adventure to experience the unknown rests with our astronauts and scientists, who have made it possible to travel beyond our planet and, with telescopes, reach further into the firmament to the beginning of time.

The merchants of this history were little different from us today. They aspired to venture beyond the known, further their position in life, seek success, provide an education for their children. They enjoyed the cultural arts, the written word and sought to understand the world within which they lived. The children of these merchants had to grow up quickly. At school they worked under a more robust and disciplined regime than some today but in several ways they behaved as children do now. There is evidence among future generations that their offspring could be just as difficult when thwarted as ours can be. Exhortations to marry a chosen suitor not to their liking met with rejection even when family coffers were at stake, causing parent and child to resort to subterfuge and sometimes causing the father political embarrassment at the highest level. The child sometimes won.

Characters and personalities remain similar. There were the selfless, the selfish, the benevolent, the untrustworthy, the thoughtful and the 'go-getters.' The men of this history were mindful of unforgiving times and a need to forge a prosperous life for themselves and those that came after them. - Most people abided by a code of conduct relating to what they considered honourable behaviour and they adhered to their faith, even if that meant death at the stake. They believed in the dignity of their calling, their traditions and the nurture of their families. They lived in a harsher world with rougher justice, torture, superstition and cruel punishment; that was the stage of understanding and civilisation the world had reached at that time. Even so, there was distaste for some events and punishments such as

Otwell Johnson's horror at the beheading of King Henry VIII's queen, the distaste for burning at the stake and the repugnance of most of the next generation at the beheading of their King.

Our ancestors were more God-fearing than are most people in Britain today. Religion played a significant part in their lives. With a myriad of dangers, disease and little medical relief, death walked beside them every day. It is understandable that in a world they did not fully comprehend, a belief in God and superstition gave hope and explanation. With threats of fire and brimstone issued from the pulpit many wills requested that prayers for redemption be said for the departed, sometimes for several years. The wills of the merchants also provide evidence of the intricate network of support cultivated amongst family and friends. They reveal an awareness and responsibility towards the less fortunate and consideration for those that served their family and business. The Tudors knew that the hand of fate could impoverish anyone through no fault of their own. Untimely death, illness, bad luck or the malfeasance of others could bring disaster and destitution, so wills often instructed that the debts of prisoners be paid and bequests be given to the poor and sick of the parish, to hospitals and charities and the orphaned.

Poverty was still a problem and the City barely coped with the influx of rural people and aliens into London. Nevertheless, prospects improved for a greater number of people. The creation of companies to colonise America and other lands gave hope, opportunity and investment potential to those who ventured there and managed to survive against the considerable difficulties. The foundation of the East India Company enhanced trade overseas for years to come.

It was still necessary to create assets, protect inheritance and maintain prosperity, hence the second generation capitalised on the success of their fathers. They now had the resources to sustain them through the divisive upheaval that lay ahead and to forge a different path if they chose. The eldest Whitmore son, Sir William, studied law, engaged in property speculation and became the first in a long line of family politicians, and his descendants continued to live for centuries at Apley Park in Shropshire and Lower Slaughter Manor, Gloucestershire. The second son, Thomas, died and the third, Sir George, chose a civic life within the aldermanry. He became a director of the East India Company followed by a year as lord mayor of London. Both sons invested in the newly-formed trading companies and were ardent supporters of the monarchy though aware of the Stuart monarchs flaws.

Their Bourman cousins of the seventeenth century furthered the discovery and expansion of new markets in the Caribbean, Africa and

America and the Spanish blood of Hugh and Simon proved useful to the English merchants of the Stuart era. Hugh held a diplomatic post as consul to San Lucar and Seville, which it was hoped would facilitate trading agreements between Britain and Spain. Simon stood to become consul for Malaga, to aid the expansion of the port there, but a rival was elected instead.[155] Simon, therefore, continued to trade overseas and unwisely harassed the Spanish whenever opportunity arose, but then in 1606 fortunes reversed. As captain of his father's ship, the Saloman he was captured with his thirty-eight crew by the Spanish near Colombia and imprisoned. Three years later he was released on the recommendation of Spain's Council of the Indies. They described him as intelligent, Catholic, the son of a Spanish mother and as wishing to remain in the service of His Majesty, King Philip III. He was then awarded a post serving on Spain's galleys.[156] [157]

Happy in Cornwall, the somewhat eccentric Alexander Daniell put his individualistic talents to use in local matters. He chose to settle at Laregan near his father's home until his own death in 1668. He married the blue-blooded Grace Bluett in 1625 having abandoned his first choice of wife, Sara Martin, whom he met during a visit to London in 1621. His sister Mary Whitmore (Copcott) had strongly disapproved. According to Alexander's diary, '*she would not endure to hear of it.*' Big sister evidently had some clout, her influence apparently as strong as his father's during Alexander's early youth.

Alexander was a keen Calvinist and wrote a number of poems based upon his religious beliefs. His will indicates a man of learning and lists books in Latin, Greek, Spanish, French and Dutch. He died during the reign of the third Stuart king, Charles II. His tomb in Madran churchyard is marked with

---

[155] 'Introduction: The revival of the company, 1604–6', in The Spanish Company, ed. Pauline Croft (London, 1973), pp. xxix-li. *British History Online* http://www.british-history.ac.uk/london-record-soc/vol9/xxix-li accessed 24 June 2021].

[156] *The Afro-Portuguese Maritime World and The Foundations of Spanish Caribbean Society, 1570–1640* By David Wheat, Dissertation Submitted to the Faculty of the Graduate School of Vanderbilt University in partial fulfilment of the requirements for the degree in Doctor of Philosophy in History August, 2009 http://etd.library.vanderbilt.edu/available/etd-05272009-181157/unrestricted/Wheat_Dissertation.pdf.

[157] English Voyages to the Caribbean, 1596 to 1604: An Annotated List K. R. Andrews *The William and Mary Quarterly* Third Series, Vol. 31, No. 2 (Apr., 1974), pp. 243–254 (article consists of 12 pages) URL: http://www.jstor.org/stable/1920911.

the epitaph: *'Belgia*[158] *me birth, Britain me breeding gave, Cornwall a wife,*[159] *ten children, and a grave.'*

Several of Alexander's descendants chose to remain in this enchanting but relatively poor corner of England. It is the most westerly point of the British isles where the English Channel meets the Atlantic Ocean; a land of legends, smugglers, pirates and wild flowers. Only the wind hears the cry of the seabirds and bark of the seals on the uninhabited islands of its beautiful but treacherous coastline.

Several roads are named after the Daniell family and later generations achieved wealth and distinction, building a grand town house in Truro. Ralph Allen Daniell,[160] merchant, banker and MP for Looe, the son of Thomas 'Guinea a Minute' Daniell[161] bought the estate of Trelissick on the Falmouth estuary in 1805 and expanded the beautiful garden, which his son, Thomas enhanced with trees and shrubs. It is now a major tourist attraction further developed by later owners after the younger Thomas Daniell became insolvent.[162]

William Bond, grandson of the merchant adventurer William Bond, continued the mercantile tradition of the family. He died in 1671 leaving a detailed will. Unmarried, he was the last in the male line of his side of the Bond family, although there are descendants through his Whitmore cousins. The male Bond line, therefore, continued through the descendants of Sir George Bond and the Dorset and Cornish Bonds. Sir Thomas Bond, descended from Sir George, became controller of the household of Queen Henrietta Maria, wife of Charles I. He was also the developer of Bond Street, London, named after him.

The activities of John Bond from the Dorset branch supplied the Bond family motto 'Orbis non sufficit', 'The World is not Enough': words that befit the wanderlust of the Bond adventurers. It was the motto of the Spanish king, purloined by John Bond in jest and scorn. He spotted the motto in 1589 during a mission with Sir Francis Drake to capture the Azores from the

---

[158] Born in Middelburg, a municipality, a city in the south eastern Netherlands and the capital of Zeeland.

[159] *The Cornish Family* by Bernard Deacon & Autobiography of Alexander Daniel of Alverton 1599–1688 – Journal of the Royal Institution of Cornwall NS7 (1977) 262-75.

[160] Descended from William Daniell MP for Truro, second son of Richard Daniel, half-brother to Alexander Daniell

[161] Cornwall Record Office

[162] The History of Ewyas-Lacy http://www.ewyaslacy.org.uk/-/Riches-to-Rags-The-Bankruptcy-of-Thomas-Daniell-of-Michaelchurch-Court-Lord-of-the-Manor-of-Ewyas-Lacy-By-Bob-Steele/1835-1851/rs_ewy_0137

Spanish,[163] who had recently bought them from the Portuguese. Such an emotive motto fires the imagination and it became the title of the 1999 James Bond film, starring Piers Brosnan.

In the twentieth century, the travails of that time brought sorrow to this Dorset branch of the family living in the Domesday village of Tyneham. In 1943 Sir Winston Churchill's government commandeered their estate and the homes of their tenants for use as a firing range and the training ground for World War II troops. All the residents had to leave. The Bond home, Tyneham House, had been in the family since 1683 and the church contained many family monuments. The last person to leave the village in 1943 left this poignant message on the church door.

'Please treat the church and houses with care; we have given up our homes where many of us lived for generations to help win the war to keep men free. We shall return one day and thank you for treating the village kindly.'

Heartfelt sorrow and a modest wish. The little community had left with hope for the future, unaware that they had stepped over their thresholds for the last time. Despite a promise to the Bond family and the villagers, their homes were never restored to them. Today, the ghost village exists as a time warp, a reminder of all that was sacrificed in terms of life, land and occupation, so that the rest of us could live in peace and safety.[164]

Whereas curtailing the danger from the French and Spanish Catholic nations had occupied the attention of Queen Elizabeth, the constant struggle between Protestant England and the nations of the Roman Catholic faith had determined the lives and actions of the merchant adventurers of the sixteenth century. In the mid-seventeenth century their children and grandchildren faced one of the most turbulent and divisive events of English history. Each family had a tale to tell.

People became increasingly exasperated when King Charles I believed his 'divine right' as King trumped the role of Parliament and the Magna Carta, which states that neither monarch nor subjects are above the law. The king's intransigence polarised the nation leading to the English Civil War as did the Puritans suppression of those of a different faith. Royalists believed the established monarchy and right of succession best served the country, but

---

[163] The motto used by Sir Thomas Bond Bt, descendant of Sir George Bond, William's brother, was used by both the Somerset and Dorset branch.
http://en.wikipedia.org/wiki/List_of_James_Bond_title_references

[164] *Tyneham: A Lost Heritage* [Paperback] by Lilian Bond

others sided with the Parliamentarians wish for a democratic Puritan republic.

The resultant civil strife caused loss of life, despoiling of places of worship, damage to historic buildings and homes and division in families. The losing Royalists had to pay vast sums for retrieval of their sequestered property while the successful but puritanical Parliamentarians created a censorious existence largely devoid of levity, entertainment and ecclesiastic beauty. What happened and who prevailed in the end belongs to another story.

Notes

[i] **Margaret Baynham** The relationship between Margaret Baynham and the Planckney family is not clear, but she writes of her sister Planckney. The circumstantial evidence indicates that she was the daughter of William Lynn(e) and sister of Elizabeth Planckney. Also, Margaret's first husband may have been one of the Planckneys. In a letter, Henry Southwick describes Margaret Baynham as John Johnson's aunt, but on what basis is not known. Henry Southwick's will of 1551 appears to indicate that Margaret Baynham was his aunt also. Margaret Baynham's step-daughter married William Saxby and that family was related to the Johnson family.

[ii] **Frances Whitmore** Frances, wife of Richard Whitmore is sometimes wrongly named as Frances Baker. She became Frances Barker after her second marriage to William Barker of Aston, Shropshire. Her maiden name is not recorded in the family tree but a booklet in the Gloucestershire archives D45/F37 for the Whitmore family records her as Frances Knotte, the daughter of Thomas Knotte of Claverley. *Genealogical Notes on Whitmores of Apley* by Mary Russell

[iii] **William Whitmore, Merchant Adventurer** Some genealogies erroneously record William Whitmore as born in 1545. This does not fit in with any of the known facts of his life. It also means that all of the ensuing 'data' in these online genealogies are incorrect. That date does not fit with the date or terms of his father's will of 1549, which indicates that William was already an adult, probably around twenty-four. Some also state that William Whitmore married Eleanor Troble of Somerset. This is not true. There are no documents recording such a marriage. William Whitmore from Shropshire did not marry anyone other than Ann Bond. Some have also stated that each of his children were born in different locations from each other. This too is wrong. Apart from his rarely visited estate in Shropshire, William lived and worked in considerable comfort in London. No-one of his status in Tudor England, with business and city obligations would be roaming around the country.

[iv] **Ann Bond** Some genealogy sites erroneously report that Robert King(e) was the second husband of Ann Bond. He was her first husband in a short-lived marriage. He died in 1569. His nuncupative will (oral or written by someone else later) and proved in 1570 mentions his wife Ann. There were no children of the King marriage. Ann's date of birth is variously reported as 1545 and 1557. At the later date of 1557, she would have been less than 12 years old when married to Robert King. Since her parents married around 1549/50 it is likely that she was born between 1549–1553. It was unusual for the children of these families to marry before their late teens

or older, unless it was a betrothal i.e. with the intention that a marriage should take place at a later date... The London Port Book for March-May 1568 records a Robert King trading with the Netherlands using the ships the Swallow and Mary Fortune of Lee. Ann's father and uncle, William and George Bond were trading at the same time, which, no doubt, is how Ann came to know Robert King.

[v] **William Bond – Merchant Adventurer** His birth has been recorded in some quarters as ca. 1529 but if his marriage was between 1545 and 1550 that would make him sixteen in 1545 or twenty/twenty-one in 1549/50 when he married Margaret Aldy. The rules of the livery companies forbade marriage before the age of twenty-four. Therefore, William is most likely to have been born around 1524/25 as stated in other sources. He is unlikely to have been born earlier since his parents William Bond of Buckland, Somerset and Dionese Bourman were married in 1523. We know from his epitaph and memorial that he had six sons and one daughter of which four sons and a daughter survived and that he had many adventures overseas. A deceased son, John Bennet was born round 1550.

[vi] **Aldy family** Margaret Aldy was born around 1529. Although Margaret's lineage has not come to light, it is indicated by her coat of arms and can be deduced. The will of Thomas Aldy d. 1534 who married Bennet Exhurst appears to indicate that her father, William Aldy, was one of his brothers and that William also had a son, Henry Allday. According to the will of Thomas Aldy, Nicholas Aldy was Margaret's grandfather: Bennet Exhurst was the great-granddaughter of Thomas Ellis, the founder of St. Thomas's Hospital in Sandwich.

[vii] **William Bond the younger** The children of William Bond the younger and Margaret Gore were christened at St. Stephen's church, Walbrook between 1582 and 1595. One son, registered as George in 1595 may be the son named Gore. There are several Bonds within the register and many will be the sons and daughters of other members of the family.

[vix] **Copcott** The evidence for the fraternity of Reynold and John Copcott comes from the will of Alice Hampton (nee Planckney), their half-sister, and the will of Reynold, who bequeaths money to Bennet College (now named Christ College) and Trinity College, both colleges of Cambridge University attended by his brother. John died in 1590, hence Reynold's bequest to his brother's colleges. Since the age of entrance to Cambridge University was around sixteen/seventeen and apprenticeships usually started at the age of fourteen, Reynold may have been the younger brother born around 1553. However, the usual date given for his birth is about 1546. Actual dates for these brothers births have not been found.

Index

Aldy, Margaret 27, 36, 53, 77, 82
Aldy, Thomas 39
Aldy, John 39
Aldy, William 39
al-Ghalib, Sultan Abdullah 61
Algerine Pirates 103
Allday, Henry 39
Alva, Duke of 48
Anglican Catholic Church of England 14
Antwerp 11, 40, 41, 90
Antwerp staple 3
Apley Hall 26
Apley Park 26, 28, 34
Archangel 45
Baffin Island 59
Balmes Estate 23
Barbary Company 60
Barbary Pirates 42
Barker, Frances 23
Barker, Francis 23, 30
Barker, John 23, 30
Barker, William 23, 30
Barker, William Jr. 23
Bartholomew's Hospital 79
Bateman, Robert 79
Baynham, Margaret 6, 87
Baynham, Robert 6, 87
Berkshire 38
Beston (Beeston), Sir George 72, 75
Billingsley, Richard 9
Birkman/Kirkham, Joan 37
Bladwell, John 21, 30
Bladwell, Robert 30
Blandings Castle 26
Bluett, Grace 107
Blundell, Peter 17, 21, 30, 31, 33, 34
Blundell's School 17, 33
Bobbington 9, 15
Boleyn, Ann 13
Bond(e), Margarett 44
Bond, Ann 27, 40
Bond, Daniel 40

Bond, Gore 61
Bond, John 54, 89, 108
Bond, Margaret 6, 56
Bond, Martin 17, 27, 33, 40, 54, 71, 72, 77, 78, 79, 80, 81, 82
Bond, Nicholas 40, 77
Bond, Robert 38
Bond, Robert of Trull 37
Bond, Sir George 27, 37, 40, 47, 57, 64, 65, 66, 67, 71, 72, 108
Bond, Sir Thomas 108
Bond, Sir William 28
Bond, Thomas 55, 79
Bond, William 2, 6, 27, 33, 34, 36, 37, 40, 41, 43, 47, 48, 49, 50, 51, 52, 53, 54, 55, 57, 59, 63, 64, 67, 72, 77, 84, 89, 108
Bond, William (son of the younger) 61
Bond, William (the younger) 40, 57, 58, 60, 61, 66, 67
Bourman (Bowreman), Henry of Chard 76
Bourman, Dionese 36, 37
Bourman, Hugh 107
Bourman, Isabel 71, 73, 76
Bourman, James 63
Bourman, John 37, 63
Bourman, Simon (senior) 34, 57, 63, 64, 66, 67, 68, 69, 70, 71, 76
Bourman, Simon (the younger) 107
Bourman, William MP 64
Bowdler, Agnes 10
Bowreman, Joan 37
Boys, Jane 56
Boys, Sir John 56
Brideswell Hospital 32
Bridgnorth 11, 26
British Federation of University Women 49
Brook, Isle of Wight 37, 63
Bruges 11
Bruskin, Raf 30
Buckingham, Duke of 104
Buckland, Somerset 36
Bull, Thomas 94

Burning fever 97
Burnsall School 17
Cabeça, Isaac 61
Cabot, Sebastian 43
Cadiz 25, 67
Calais 11, 39, 87
Calvanist 86
Capcott/Copcott, John 87
Carvanell, Isobel 63
Cathay (China) 42
Catholicism 86
Cave, Anthony 3
Cecil, Sir Robert 90, 98, 100
Cecil, William 3
Chancellor, Richard 43, 44, 45, 47
Christ's Hospital 29, 32
Churchill, Sir Winston 109
Claverley 7, 9, 13, 15, 22
Claverley, All Saints Church 15
Clutterbooke, Fernando 88
Cockayne, William 102
Collimore, Francis 100
Collimore, Justus 104
Collimore, Robert 100
Colombia 107
Columbus, Christopher 9
Company of Haberdashers 16
Company of Ironmongers 88, 93
Company of Merchant Adventurers 32
Company of Merchant Adventurers for the Discovery of Regions, Dominions, Islands and Places Unknown 43
Compton, Lord 81
Comptor prison 32
Copcott, Adam 87, 88
Copcott, John 88, 93
Copcott, Mary 97, 98, 99, 100, 101
Copcott, Reynold 2, 34, 86, 87, 88, 90, 92, 96, 97, 98, 100, 101
Copuldyke 39
Cornwall 38
Crant, John 87
Crante, Thomas 94
Craven, Lady Elizabeth 6, 80
Craven, Lord William 56, 80
Craven, Sir William 16, 21, 56
Creech, Dorset 37
Cromwell, Oliver 52, 104

Cromwell, Thomas 13
Crosby Hall 57
Crosby Moran Hall 35, 50, 57
Crosby Place 49, 51, 53, 54
Crosby, John 49
Crosse, Robert 68
Culm Davy, Hemyock 63
d'Assonleville 50, 51
d'Erth, Elizabeth 38
d'Erth, Sir Geoffrey 38
Daniell, Alexander 96
Daniell, Alexander Jr. 97, 99, 101, 103, 107
Daniell, George 17
Daniell, Ralph Allen 108
Daniell, Richard 17, 34, 94, 98, 99, 101, 102, 103
Daniell, T.B. Jenken 101
Daniell, Thomas 108
Daniell, Thomas 'Guinea a Minute' 108
Davison, William 92
de Spes, Don Guerau 50
Dee, John 44, 60
Denison, Stephen 80
Diet at Augsberg 90
Dorset 38
Drake, Sir Francis 57, 68, 72, 74, 108
Drapers' Company 96, 102
Dudley, Robert, Earl of Leicester 86
Dutch Revolt 96
East India Company 61, 80, 106
Eastland Company 53
Edmondes, Thomas 100
Edric Sylvaticus (the wild) 8
Elizabeth I, Queen 50, 51, 58, 65, 67, 75, 89
Elizabeth, Queen of Bohemia 80
Finch, Sir Heneage 79
Fishborne, Nicholas 55
Fleet prison 47
Forest of Dean 73
Foster, Mr. 67
Four Members of Flanders 89
Foxall, John 47, 55
France 24
Francois I, King of France 87
Frederick V, Elector 80
Friesland 59, 60
Frobisher Bay 60
Frobisher, Martin 58, 59, 60, 68

INDEX

Gage, Sir John 1
Ganeghan, van Margaret 99
Gardener, John 30
Gataker, Thomas 33
Gayer, Sir John 80
Gilpin, George 90, 91
Gils d'Avila, Isabel 64
Glapthorne estate 3
Gore, Gerard 60
Gore, Margaret 53, 60
Gore, Thomas 60
Gore, Thomas & Gerard 61
Great Companies, The 20
Greenland 59
Gresham, Thomas 23, 54
Grey, Lady Jane 13
Guildford, Sir Edward 39
Guise, Mary of 15
Gyles, Stephen 64, 70
Haberdashers' Aske's Schools 16
Haberdashers' Company 11, 32, 40
Hall's Island 60
Hampton (Planckney), Alice 94
Hampton, Christopher Archbishop of Armagh 94, 98, 101
Hampton, Francis 94, 98
Hampton, John 100
Hamptons 98
Hansa 90
Hanseatic League 40, 41
hantavirus pulmonary syndrome 3
Harald Fairhair, King 37
Hardres, Sir Thomas 80
Harrison, Roger 19
Harvey, Thomas 61
Harvey, William 79
Hatton, Sir Christopher 26, 55
Hawkins, John 42, 67, 72
Hemyock 37
Henrietta Maria, Queen 108
Hitler, Adolf 26
Hoegaerden, van Abraham 93
Hoegaerden, van Baptista 93
Hoegaerden, van Clara 93
Hoegaerden, van Jacquelina 93, 97, 100
Hoep, Matthias 77
Holdenby 26
Honourable Artillery Company 79, 89

Hopton 9
Howe, Henry 63
Howe, Roger 66, 67, 68
Incledon, Robert Newton 34
Industrial Revolution 9
Inuit 59
Ironbridge 9
Ivan IV, Tsar 45
James I, King 31, 61, 77, 78, 80, 102
John, Sir Spencer 81
Johnson, Edward 3
Johnson, John 1, 2, 3, 4, 6, 87
Johnson, Otwell 2, 4, 106
Johnson, Richard 3, 5
Johnson, Sabine 2, 6, 54
Jones, Francis 16
Jones, Sir Francis 16, 30
Jones' Grammar School 80
Katherine of Aragon 13
Keynsham Manor 31
King Harald Fairhair 37
King, Robert 27
King's College, Cambridge University 28
King's Merchant Adventurers 102
Kirby Hall 26
Knott, Frances 9
Knott, Thomas 9
Knotte, John 9
Knotte, Richard 9
Labrador 59
Laird of Poltalloch 76
Landreau, Captain (Pirate) 55
Laregan 107
Leicester, Earl of 72
Leiden University 103
Levant Company 61
Lewis, Joan 30
Lincoln College Oxford 102
Llwyd, Humphrey 44
Lok, Michael 59, 60
London 11, 33, 38
London Trained Bands 71
London, Dr. John 13, 14
Lübeck 77
Lucas de Campos 51
Lucy, Sir Thomas 26
Ludgate prison 32
Ludstone 9, 16

INDEX

Ludstone Hall 10
Luis, Bernaldo 69, 70
Luther, Martin 15
Lyne, Edward 31
Lynn(e), Elizabeth 87
Machievelli 13
Madron school 17
Malaga 64
Malcolm, Colonel Edward Donald 76
Marco Polo 24, 42
Marlborough, 1st Duke 40
Marrakesh 60
Marranos 70
Martin, Sara 107
Martin. Sir Roger 48
Mary I, Queen 2, 13, 46, 47
Mary, Queen of Scots 13, 15, 89
Medici Bank of London 5
Medina Sidona, Duke de 73
Meghen, van Maria 93, 98, 103
Melbourne, Viscount 40
Mendoza, de Bernardino 64, 65, 69
Merchant Taylors' Company 88
Michiel, Giovanni 46
Middelburg 11, 87, 96
Middle Temple 28, 56
Middleton, Sir Thomas 79
Monmouth School for Girls 80
Moran, Dr Christopher 50
More, Sir Thomas 49
Moscow 45
Muscovy Company 44, 45, 58
Mussel, Mr. 79
Narva 47
Naunton, James 69
Naylor, William 19
Nazi headquarters 26
Nelson, Admiral Horatio 74
Netherlands 41, 48, 50, 92, 96
Netherlands- Iconoclasm 86
Netherlands Revolt 48
Newgate prison 29
Northeast Passage 54, 58
Northwest Passage 58
Nunez, Dr Hector. 69, 70
Okes, William 30
Operation Sealion 26
Pagit, Ephraim 33

Palmer, Valentine 92
Paracelsus 13
Pardo, Geronimo 69, 70
Parker, William 21
Pepys, Samuel 24
Philip II, King 86
Planckney, Alice 3, 94, 100
Planckney, Daniel 94
Planckney, Edward 14, 87
Planckney, Henry 14, 94, 99
Planckney, Margery 87
Playa d'Agadir 60
Plymouth 72
Polstead, Henry 21, 30, 33, 97
Poole, William 74
Portuguese 25
Prouninck, Gerhard 89
Puerto de Santa Maria 25
Queen Elizabeth Foreland 59
Ramelius, Henry 54
Richard III, King 49
Rosehearty, Aberdeen 46
Rowe, Sir Thomas 48
Rubens 104
Russell, Francis 68
Russell, John 1st Earl of Bedford 41
Russia 58
Russia Company 44, 47, 48, 53
Salde, de la Katherine 64
San Lucar de Barrameda 25
Sandwich 39
Santa Croce, Admiral 73
Santa Cruz, Pedro 69, 70
Saunders, Blaise 2, 3, 54
Saunders, Laurence 2, 4
Saunders, Sabine 2, 3, 6
Savoy, Duke of 67
Sephardic Jews 70
Seville 25, 51, 64, 69
Seville Inquisition 52
Shakespeare 49, 61
Shrewsbury 11
Sidona, Duke de Medina 74
Sluis 39
Smith, Sir John 64
Somers Island Company 78
Somerset 38, 52
Spain 11, 24, 50, 75

INDEX

Spanish and Portuguese Company 25
Spanish Armada 13, 27, 28, 40, 68, 71, 72, 75
Spanish Company 25, 61, 78
Spanish Fury 86
Spanish Inquisition 51
Spanish Netherlands 41
Spanish Riding School 13
Spencer, Sir John 54
Spindlowe, Mr. 33
St Katherine Cree 80
St. Alban Hall 77
St. Alban's College 54
St. Aldegonde 91, 92
St. Andrews Undershaft 81
St. Anthony's school 28
St. Bartholomew Day Massacre 89
St. Bartholomew's Hospital 32
St. Edmund, King and Martyr 27
St. Erth 38
St. Thomas's Hospital 32
Stade 11, 77
Steelyard 40, 41
Stelan 65
Still, John 72
Sweating Sickness 2, 3, 97
Tilbury 73, 75
Tiverton School 17
Trained Bands of London 72, 77
Treaty of Nonsuch 86
Trinity College Cambridge 72
Trumbull, William 100
Turkey Company 61
Tyneham, Dorset 37, 109
United Provinces 90
Valverde, Francisco 69, 70, 73
van Dyke 104
Viking Bonders of Norway 37
Virginia Company 61, 78
Viroconium Cornoviorum 8

Wake, Lionel 100
Walcheren 96
Walker, Jane 56
Walsingham, Sir Francis 3, 34, 67, 69, 71, 90, 92
Weld, Lady Frances 6
Weld, Sir Humphrey 79
Werke, Vander (van der) 91
West Monmouthshire School 80
Wheeler, J. 98
Whitgift, John (Archbishop of Canterbury) 88
Whitmore, Ann (nee Bond) 31
Whitmore, Frances 23, 79
Whitmore, George 103
Whitmore, Mary (Copcott) 107
Whitmore, Richard 11, 14, 22, 23
Whitmore, Sir George 24, 32, 80, 97, 101, 103, 104, 106
Whitmore, Sir William 23, 31, 34, 79
Whitmore, Sir Willian 106
Whitmore, Thomas 9, 23, 34, 106
Whitmore, William 3, 6, 7, 9, 13, 16, 17, 19, 20, 21, 22, 23, 24, 25, 27, 28, 29, 32, 33, 34, 36, 40, 43, 51, 54, 56, 57, 68, 69, 71, 84, 86, 103, 104
Whitmore, William of Balmes, Middlesex 88
Whittemere 9
Whytmere, de John 9, 22
Whytmere, de Richard 7, 9, 10
Wilkinson, John 74
William Jones Haberdasher School 79
William of Orange 50, 96
William, Lord Craven 24
William, Prince of Orange 96
Willoughby, Sir Hugh 43, 44, 47
Winchester, Barbara 4
Winter, Sir William 72
Wodehouse, P.G. 26
Wroxeter 8

Lightning Source UK Ltd.
Milton Keynes UK
UKHW051105060223
416527UK00011B/430